Games, Giggles, and Giant Steps

written by Susan Miller, ED.D.
illustrated by Patty Briles

Author, Susan Miller; Editor, Christine Van Huysse; Illustrator, Patty Briles; Designer, Caroline Foster; Cover Design, Laurie Semmens; Copy Editors, John Nemec, Anne Marie DiTeodoro; Graphics Coordinator, David Komitau; Production Managers, Kathy Edquist, Jeanne Johnson, Andrea Junker; The Instructor Books Staff: Ben Miyares, Director; Barbara Michel, Manager.

CONTENTS

ACKNOWLEDGMENTS

Foremost, to Gregg, my son, for whom many of these games were created and his father, Peter, who enjoyed playing them with us.

To the countless teachers and parents throughout the country who shared games at conferences and workshops. In particular, to Cynthia Curtis at Amherst College for a *Sound Story.* To the numerous Kutztown University Early Learning Center children, their parents, early childhood education students, and kindergarten supervisor, Sandra Fisher, who helped to develop, play, and refine various games.

To the Kutztown University Research Committee, which lent its support to this project, along with Karen Epting, my typist and Karen Hamm, my research assistant.

A very special thank you to the laboratory school faculty members and directors at Southeast Missouri State University, Southwest Baptist University, Vassar College, and Worcester State College for field-testing selected games and offering valuable suggestions.

To INSTRUCTOR editors, Judy Cohn, Jane Schall, and Nancy-Jo Hereford, for their encouragement, ideas, and patience. To Edgell Communications editors Anne Marie Di Teodoro, for her assistance, and Chris Van Huysse, for her caring and professionalism. To Patty Briles for her delightful illustrations of children that add so much to the games.

To INSTRUCTOR's Early Childhood Teacher magazine for permission to reprint this author's copyrighted games: *Bubble Dancing, From Here to There,* and *Me and My Shadow.*

Susan Anderson Miller, Ed.D.
Kutztown University of Pennsylvania

INTRODUCTION

Games, Giggles, and Giant Steps is chock-full of child-tested games, some traditional, others original, played, developed, and enjoyed with preschoolers and primary children during my past 25 years of teaching and parenting. As an early childhood teacher, director, resource consultant, writer, editor, and professor, I have had many wonderful occasions to share these educationally sound games with parents and teachers, always learning unique ones in return. I quickly discovered, as the mother of an active, inquisitive, adventuresome preschooler (now a college student), the value of having instant games at my fingertips to draw upon while we traveled, waited, laughed, hugged, and played together.

The games which follow are designed to meet the developmental levels, needs, and interests of young children, late-toddler through primary (ages 2 through 8). As you become familiar with these activities, which do not require equipment, it soon becomes apparent that expensive materials are not necessary; simply draw upon your, and the children's, creative resources. Most of these practical games can be played during a short time in a limited space—a bonus for both teachers and parents!

The games collected here are grouped by categories as well as cross-referenced on page 158 for teaching ease. The games offer opportunities for adults and children to spend creative time together, stretching imaginations and testing ingenuity in the spirit of contagious fun! In today's fast-paced world, the close contact, spontaneity, and comradery involved in playing games together is so important. I hope that you, too, will enjoy these games with your special children.

THE VALUE OF GAME PLAYING

Throughout time, children have played games: traditional ones handed down by parents and teachers and others originated by the children themselves. Games are played alone, with peers, and with very special adults. Sometimes games are played for the learning experience, other times for sheer enjoyment. This type of play, integral in childhood, enhances development in the following ways:

1. The playing of games naturally strengthens language, listening, math, science, social studies, sensory, motor, memory, and judgment skills. Young children learn best and enjoy it most when they practice these skills through active play.

2. Cognitive growth is stimulated as players encounter unfamiliar situations, gather information, and apply it to new experiences. Games provide opportunities for problem solving and critical thinking.

3. Through games, children emphasize individualism and creativity as they explore, discover, and experiment.

4. Game playing in a comfortable environment encourages children to increase language development and proficiency in verbalizing thoughts.

5. In playing games, children develop confidence, self-control, and independence; they learn to experiment with risks and take initiative.

6. Imagination is fostered as children dramatize, pretend, and role play—expressing the thoughts and gestures of many characters, real, unusual, or imagined!

7. Mastery skills are developed in learning to follow step-by-step directions and rules.

8. The concentration required to participate in games is a wonderful way to increase attention spans.

9. Through exploration, the youngsters are challenged to focus upon, manipulate, and coordinate body movements.

10. An appreciation of music and a sense of rhythm are acquired as children participate in games, songs, and chants.

11. Games allow youngsters an opportunity to relax and have fun with others and release anxiety or tension.

12. Cooperation with others, sharing ideas, turn-taking, and social skills are learned.

13. Game playing contributes to a child's knowledge of other people and the world about, as well as an awareness of the self operating within that environment.

14. Positive adult/child relationships and interactions are augmented as games are played together.

15. Children receive support as they work through difficult situations. Through game play, it is possible to rehearse responses to and role play specific circumstances (emergency phone calls, a child lost in the park, or positive interactions with others).

STRATEGIES FOR GAME PLAYING

Playing games with children can be lots of fun. If simple management and playing strategies are employed, the games can be enjoyable for everyone. The following are successful tactics that, over the years, have been found extremely helpful.

1. Give directions clearly and simply so that the players know the objectives of the game. Model new skills for the children, then allow them adequate practice to feel comfortable.

2. Match the games with appropriate developmental levels and interests. Modify games by making them easier or harder; apply variations and pertinent adaptations to challenge the players or relieve frustration. Each game in this book is marked for easy reference. Letters in parentheses after a skill (E,H,V,A) let you know which version (Easier, Harder, Variation, Adaptation) practices or develops a particular skill.

3. Take into account individual differences (shyness, high or low self-esteem, and so forth) and learning style modalities (visual, auditory, kinesthetic, mixed) for enhancing optimum performances.

4. Establish rules that players can be comfortable with for touching and holding. Melissa Greig, Vassar College preschool teacher, states, ''It is important to respect a child's body. Ask permission to touch or hold a child on your lap for a game. In this way, discussions of privacy begin very naturally.''

5. Be a partner to a child who needs extra assistance or pair this player with a child who has mastered the skill.

6. To develop positive self-images, use children's names frequently. Praise often with winks, pats, or comments such as: *great!*, *nice idea!*, or *wonderful job!*

7. If a youngster can't think of a response, tell the player that you'll come back to him or her later, then don't forget. (Give hints when appropriate.)

8. Make sure that young children have many opportunities to replay favorite, familiar games. Children love repetition; it furthermore enhances self-confidence as children perfect skills already developed.

9. Give the players a choice only when you want them to have one. For the most part, use statements, not questions; say, for example: *Hold hands and make a circle,* instead of, *Do you want to form a circle now?*

10. Establish ground rules and make sure children understand them. Use statements such as: *if someone misses a response, the play begins again; a player is allowed two guesses; the boundaries are between the fence and the elm tree.*

11. If you are comfortable with using them, determine simple controlling devices and explain to the children how these signals will be used. The signal *to stop* or *listen* might be *a clap of the hands* or *a blink of the lights.*

12. Give children ample time to play so they don't feel pressured or hurried.

13. Check play areas for hazards, such as loose rugs or broken glass.

14. Allow plenty of room to eliminate crowding and encourage the exploration of space.

15. Utilize creative game designs for variety. Have players vary their formations *(partner, line, line and leader, circle, circle and leader, scattered)*. Change their methods of movement *(gallop, skip)* or boundaries *(the walls, rug area)*.

16. Vary the tempo of the games; use quiet and active games, familiar and new ones. Proceed from simple games to those that are more complex.

17. If a child is eliminated as part of the play, have him or her sit out only one turn or evolve into another role. This keeps all youngsters involved throughout the game.

18. Switch leader and follower roles often so that particular children do not dominate the game. Emphasize giving everyone who wants to play a chance.

19. To keep interest high, make sure the game moves along. If necessary, divide a large group into two smaller ones or designate several players instead of one as *It*. Substitute another game if one slows down or becomes too complicated.

20. Whenever possible, ask the players open-ended questions that encourage creative responses.

21. Most important, your sincere enthusiasm for game playing is contagious—get involved, enjoy the game, and the children will as well!

THE GAME PLAN

Here's how to put the games in this book to use. Several categories are utilized to describe each game. First, the **title** reflects what the game is about. Then, whatever skills the game **develops** or practices are delineated. Many games relate to a unit of study, for example, the concept of shapes, enhancing social skills, or visual discrimination.

The next category, **audience**, states whether the activity is appropriate for toddlers, preschool, kindergarten, or primary. **Group size** describes the number of children who participate, whether individual, pairs, small or large groups. Under this category, *pair play* refers to two children or an adult and child.

Often, a game is designed with a specific **setting** or area in mind. A game may be perfect for circle time or work well in the gymnasium; a particular activity may be appropriate for snack time, transitions, or a rainy day!

Directions are listed in clear simple steps. As the children play a particular game, observe them and write notes about techniques, suggestions, and tips that worked well. To individualize for developmental levels or to challenge players, an **easier** and **harder** version are often described.

Each **variation** extends, adds a unique twist, or relates to a specific teaching unit. Often a slight change, perhaps in the type of locomotion or the intricacy of the rules, is presented. An **adaptation** enables the game users to provide for individual differences, for players who are bilingual, physically challenged, and those with visual or auditory impairments.

Not all categories may be appropriate for every game, so go ahead, personalize your own! A game framework is provided on page 12; use this reproducible with your children to develop original ideas for games at home or in school. Then be sure to share these heartwarming, laughter-inducing ideas with family members or classmates. You'll find that games in many situations— whether at home or school; while waiting, playing, laughing, or hugging; while traveling in a boat, car, plane, or train—are sure to furnish many cherished moments for youngsters and the young-at-heart.

MAKE YOUR OWN GAME

Game:

Develops:

Audience:

Group Size:

Setting:

Directions:

Easier:

Harder:

Variation:

Adaptations:

Game Designer: _____

Frequently, a teacher is asked to present an in-service workshop for other teachers, a pre-service workshop for new staff members, or a session for parents. A program of games readily lends itself to such a workshop.

Learning to play a few quick games that do not require any equipment helps adults feel comfortable when faced with difficult transition times with youngsters. It is exciting for parents and teachers to become familiar with ways to provide positive, quality, educational experiences for children as they work, wait, travel, or play together.

To ensure that the adults are at ease and relaxed enough to participate in the games, provide sets of colored name tags or ones in special shapes (squares, moons, stars, apples). In this way, no one feels singled out when *all of the red apples* are asked to join in a game.

It is important for the adults to actually play in order to experience the games through the eyes of children. Several warm-up activities aid in breaking the ice and fostering a congenial atmosphere. For example, ask the audience, *How many of you have asked a child TO WAIT JUST A MINUTE before responding to him or her?* Of course, everyone has at least once. Ask, *Do you have any idea how long a minute is?* Request that all of the players close their eyes on the signal *Go* and stand up when a minute has passed. Most players rise well before the time and are surprised that a minute is so long! (Several excellent ice-breakers in this book are: *Hey, Look Me Over!* page 78, *Clap a Pattern,* page 98; *Whisper,* page 93; and, *Follow the Leader/Mirror Game,* page 47)

The workshop leader should utilize games from various categories in this book that are appropriate for children's developmental levels and interests. Check the index, page 160, and cross-references, page 159, for games in particular categories. Be sure to leave time for participants to relate old favorites and other games they have created with their children. Whenever possible, reproduce the form in this book on page 12; use it to write out your ideas and compile them to enjoy later or share with those unable to attend the workshop.

JUST FOR FUN

These games enable the players to tune into each other one-on-one for a wonderful, quiet time together or as a playful group. Some of the games are designed to distract or cheer up players who need special nurturing and lots of hugs! Many of these activities are great tension releasers, allowing the children time to laugh and be silly. All of these games are entertaining and just plain fun!

Tickle games

Develops: alertness to sensory cues
body awareness
sequencing skills
action-word coordination
social interaction
fine motor skills
anticipation

Audience: toddler (E, V), preschool,
kindergarten

Group Size: pair or small group

Setting: circle time, transition, traveling,
language, dramatics

Directions: Sometimes youngsters need to be distracted or cheered up. Other times, they might be in a playful mood. In this game, the players soon learn to anticipate and be entertained by the gentle teasing tickle during these finger games. Repeat the following verse while the children perform the hand motions. In the first verse, the children open and shut and clap their hands. During the second, they move their fingers in a walking motion up the arm. At the end of the stanza, run the fingers down the arm.

Open, shut them; open, shut them;
give a little clap!
Open, shut them; open, shut them;
put them in your lap!
Creep them, creep them;
creep them, creep them
right up to your chin.
Open wide your little mouth—
but do not let them in!

Easier: Holding the child in your lap, move your fingers up an arm, down a leg, or over the top of the child's head while saying the verse below. Vary the mouse's speed. Allow the child to be the mouse, too!

Creepy mouse, creepy mouse, creepy mouse—
tickle you there!

Variation: Trace a finger on the child's palm as you sing the first two lines. During the last two lines, move your fingers up the arm, then tickle the child under the arm!

Round and round the garden,
like a teddy bear.
One step, two steps,
tickle you under there!

Adaptation: These games allow for a great deal of one-on-one, personal contact for the child who requires special nurturing and attention.

A mouse house

Develops: laughter
anticipation
visual awareness
listening skills
action-word coordination
social interaction

Audience: toddler (E), preschool,
kindergarten

Group Size: pair (E), small or large group

Setting: dramatics, circle time, transition,
language

Directions: Youngsters delight in little surprises and secret hiding places. In these rhymes, the mouse house is created with arms or hands.

Easier: In this fingerplay, children quickly learn to anticipate the tickle and respond with laughter. To begin, make circles on the child's palm with your index finger while you chant the first two lines. As you say the third line, move your fingers up the child's arm and, as you say the last, tickle under the arm.

> Round and round the haystack
> went the little mouse.
> One step, two steps,
> in his little house.

Harder: Say the following rhyme for young children as they act it out. First, the children make a fist with a thumb facing up and then tuck it inside the fingers. As you sing the third and fourth lines, the children move their fingers from their free hands to their lips and pantomime ''Shhhh!'' At the end of the song, the thumb pops up from the fist. Older children say the verse with you and perform the motions while awaiting the surprise ending.

> A mouse lived in a little hole,
> lived softly in a little hole.
> When all was quiet as can be,
> when all was quiet as can be,
> out popped he!

Where is Thumbkin?

Develops: familiarity with simple melodies
visual awareness
tracking and focusing skills
sequencing skills
listening skills
body awareness
social interaction
fine motor skills

Audience: toddler (E), preschool,
kindergarten

Group Size: pair, small or large group

Setting: music, circle time, transition, snack
time, language, social studies

Directions: Using the named fingers, the children sing or say this traditional fingerplay and act it out with you. At the beginning, each child puts both hands behind his or her back. As the first *Here I am* is sung, the child shows the appropriate finger on one hand. As the second *here I am* is sung, the finger on the other hand is shown. During the next two lines, the two fingers are wiggled as if talking to each other. At the last line, the fingers run away behind the back again. The song is repeated for each of the other fingers: *Pointer, Middle, Ringer,* and *Pinky.*

>   Where is (*Thumbkin*)?
>   Where is (*Thumbkin*)?
>   Here I am, here I am.
>   How are you today, sir?
>   Very well, I thank you.
>   Run away, run away.

Easier: Sit the child directly in front of you so that the child can focus on your fingers and track the action in anticipation of the next move.

Variation: The following is a good game to help the children learn each others' names. As the children sit in a circle or at the snack table, sing the *Thumbkin* song but substitute a child's name for *Thumbkin.* At the second and third lines, the youngsters point to the named child, then ask, *How are you today?* He or she responds by repeating the last two lines.

>   Where is (*Alan*)? Where is (*Alan*)?
>   Here (*Alan*) is. Here (*Alan*) is.
>   How are you today, (*Alan*)?
>   Very well, I thank you.
>   Have a nice day. Have a nice day.

Harder: Have the children close their eyes while one child hides in the room. The children sing *Where is Jan?* They try to guess her hiding place. After a while, the hidden child pops up and says, *Here I am!* If someone guesses correctly, he or she hides next.

Peek-a-boo

Develops: social interaction
visual discrimination
anticipation
awareness of others' actions
listening skills

Audience: toddler, preschool (H,V),
kindergarten (H,V)

Group Size: pair or small group

Setting: circle time, transition

Directions: For a playful game, hold a child on your lap and face the child. (Or for small group play, face the players.) Cover your eyes with your hands positioned like a barn door. Quickly, open your hands up over the eyes, as you say *peek-a-boo!* (Be sure to periodically switch roles.) This game of amusement allows the players to anticipate the peek-a-boo, laugh and be silly. It is a marvelous distraction for a grumpy child or one who needs entertaining.

Harder: 1. See if the children can keep a straight face and not laugh after they peek-a-boo. They usually cannot, which adds to the merriment!
2. When your hands open up, say *peek-a-boo*, forming a different funny face each time in order to make the players laugh. Have the children try this version, too!

Variations: 1. After you open up your hands, make a silly face which the players must try to duplicate.
2. The players cover their eyes. You change your position. For example, put an arm in the air or fold your hands in front. When you say *peek-a-boo*, the players uncover their eyes and try to match your new position.

Glad, sad or mad

Develops: visual awareness
articulating emotions
action-word coordination
comprehension of instructions
thinking skills
individuality
role reversal

Audience: toddler, preschool,
kindergarten (H), primary (V)

Group Size: pair, small (H,V)
or large group (H,V)

Setting: circle time, dramatics, transition,
or social studies

Directions: When a child looks happy, name the emotion. Reflect his or her feelings and imitate the child's facial expression or body pose. For example, smiling, say to the child: *You look happy. You have built a big block tower all by yourself.* Repeat this with other emotions. Play this game often enough for the child to become familiar with various words for feelings. Reverse roles. Relate, *I'm mad! I bumped my toe.* Make an angry-looking face and ask the child to copy it.

Harder: 1. Request that the players pantomime different emotions. Ask them to show you that they are glad, mad, or sad. For a transition game, see how quickly they can change their facial expressions as you rapidly call out *sad, mad, glad, surprised.* 2. After they have mastered dramatizing different emotions, call out an emotion: *happy.* The players then act out its opposite.

Variation: Give an example of something that makes you glad, such as seeing a beautiful colorful sunset. Have the players name a specified number of things that make them happy. Then, repeat this with other emotions.

Adaptations: Children need to learn how to express their emotions. Demonstrate acceptable ways of reacting. Point out that instead of knocking down someone's blocks, they can vent anger: stamp a foot, shake a fist, yell *I'm mad!*, or jump up and down. If a child is happy, he or she might give a hug or pat on the arm.

Muffin man

Develops: visual awareness
role alternation
familiarity with simple melodies
social interaction
awareness of self (V)
alertness to sensory cues (H)

Audience: preschool, kindergarten,
primary (V)

Group Size: small or large group

Setting: circle time, traveling (V),
social studies, music, language

Directions: The players make a circle and sing the well-known song, *The Muffin Man*. One child stands in the center with his or her eyes closed. This person is *It*. The other players circle to the left while singing. At the end of the song, *It* steps forward and touches the child in front of him or her. *It* opens his or her eyes and says, *Yes I've seen the muffin man. It's* (for example) *Jamal!* This child becomes the new *It*.

> Oh, have you seen the muffin man,
> The muffin man, the muffin man?
> Oh, have you seen the muffin man
> That lives in Drury Lane?

Harder: The person who is *It* keeps his or her eyes closed and tries to guess the child touched. Hints may be given until a correct guess is made.

Variation: In order to assist the players in learning their addresses, point to a child. This child sings along with the others. At the end of the song the selected child sings his or her address. This is a great traveling game. The players may substitute people and places to visit, such as *Grandma Adams, who lives in Millbrook, New York.*

> Have you seen Carlton Fanger,
> Carlton Fanger, Carlton Fanger?
> Have you seen Carlton Fanger
> Who lives on Eagle Street?

A personalized hokey pokey

Develops: positive self-image
visual discrimination
gross motor skills
action-word coordination
familiarity with a simple melody
listening skills

Audience: toddler (E), preschool,
kindergarten, primary

Group Size: small (E) or large group

Setting: music, circle time, social studies,
movement, self-awareness or
language

Directions: To personalize a favorite children's action song, *The Hokey Pokey,* point to a specified child in the circle. The group then sings his or her name in the song. The designated child jumps in and out of the circle as the name is sung. The other players join in and act out the chorus. The named player becomes the next leader. To keep everyone alert, the leader may vary the directions and call out *everybody, the boys,* or *the girls* instead of pointing to a particular child. The group acts out the directions accordingly.

We put Elaine in;
We take Elaine out;
Put Elaine in;
And shake her all about.

Chorus: We do the Hokey Pokey,
And we turn ourselves about.
That's what it's all about.

Easier: Encourage laughing and snuggling while singing the song in a small group. Pick up a child, put him or her in and out, and hold the child close in a rocking motion as you very gently shake the child all about.

Variations: To involve more youngsters at one time, determine categories such as: body features—*brown hair, blue eyes;* clothing worn—*shorts, tennis shoes;* or colors worn—*blue* (general), *green shirts* (specific). Substitute the appropriate suggestions in the song, for example: *We put the blue shirts in, we take the blue shirts out.*

Sing me a song

Develops: familiarity with simple melodies
listening skills
self-awareness
action-word coordination
verbal understanding
anticipation
motor skills

Audience: toddler, preschool, kindergarten

Group Size: pair or small group

Setting: music, circle time, transition,
language, self-awareness,
movement

Directions: Use familiar tunes to sing personal songs to the children. This is a wonderful way to make each youngster feel very special! Three examples are given below. In each, the players are given an opportunity to respond and follow specific directions when they hear their names. The anticipation of listening for their names keeps them alert. For these and other familiar tunes, create your own verses and movements. Let older children develop versions, too. Periodically, instead of singing one child's name, substitute *everybody*, *all of the girls*, *if you are four years old*, or other categories, or use a song to make clean-up time a game for the children.

(tune: *The Mulberry Bush*)
Laura Karch jump up and down,
Up and down, up and down.
Laura Karch jump up and down,
So early in the morning.

(tune: *Row, Row, Row Your Boat*)
Itty Chan pick up the blocks.
Put them on the shelves.
Thank you! Thank you!
Thank you! Thank you!
You are very strong!!

(tune: *Michael Row the Boat Ashore*)
David Benson close your eyes.
You did that so well!
David Benson, open your eyes.
I can see you, too!!

Adaptation: If a physically challenged child needs to exercise a specific body part, incorporate it into his or her song to make practice fun. Encourage others to join in also.

Peanut butter

Develops: language
body awareness
group consciousness
verbal understanding
sense of humor
familiarity with simple melodies
mental alertness

Audience: toddler (E), preschool,
kindergarten, primary

Group Size: individual, small or large group

Setting: circle time, snack, transition, music

Directions: Sing the following verses to the tune of *Alouetta*. The named child sings a response, touching the specified body part. If it is sensible, the child sings, for example: *Yes, I like peanut butter on my tongue.* If it is silly, the child sings, *No, I do not like peanut butter on my toes.* This favorite game allows children to laugh and be silly. They share in the amusement while waiting in anticipation for their name to be chanted. It is a wonderful way for the youngsters to learn each others' names at the beginning of the year. Repeat the song several times so everyone gets a chance to sing.

> Peanut butter, we like peanut butter.
> Peanut butter, that's the stuff for us.
> Mayan, do you like peanut butter on
> your tongue?
> (Yes) I like peanut butter on my
> tongue,
> On your tongue? On your tongue?
> (Yes) I do, (yes) I do. Ohhhh!

Easier: Touch the named child's body part while singing the lines of the song. The youngster responds by shaking his or her head yes or no.

Variations: Substitute other foods for the peanut butter, such as *spaghetti* or *scrambled eggs*. Or, have the children think up other funny items instead of peanut butter; for a really silly verse, try a *wet elephant?!*

Adaptations: Hold a very young child, or one needing special cuddling and nurturing, on your lap. Take his or her hand in yours and touch the specified body parts together as you sing the song. If English is a second language for a child, sing the word for the body part first in the native language and then sing the entire song in English.

Jingles and jiggles

Develops: laughter
anticipation
sequencing skills
rhythm
awareness of others' actions
listening skills

Audience: toddler, preschool

Group Size: pair

Setting: dramatics (H), transition,
quiet time together, language

Directions: A young child loves to bounce on an adult's knees! Place the child on your lap so that both of you are facing each other and hold hands while jiggling up and down, repeating the jingles. On the word *in*, spread your knees apart, allowing the child's bottom to drop through. Give a big hug after the child has *fallen in*. Laughter immediately follows. These are excellent bonding activities.

Easier: *Trot, Trot!*
Trot, trot to London!
Trot, trot to Spain!
Look out Sara!
You might fall in!

Harder: During the first stanza, the child is gently jiggled up and down on your knees as you chant the verse. For the second, the child is bounced up and down in a galloping motion. In the last verse, the child is bounced side to side and on the *hoy* is dropped between the knees.

This is the way the ladies ride,
tri, tre, tri, tree, tri, tre, tre, tree!
This is the way the ladies ride,
tri, tre, tre, tre, tri-tre-tre-tree!

This is the way the gentlemen ride,
gallop-a-trot, gallop-a-trot!
This is the way the gentlemen ride,
Gallop-a-gallop-a-trot!

This is the way the farmers ride,
hobbledy-hoy, hobbledy-hoy!
This is the way the farmers ride,
hobbledy-hobbledy-hoy!

Variation: Have the children dramatize the characters' rides in *This is the Way* by galloping around the play area.

Piggy fun

Develops: laughter
anticipation
sequencing skills
rhythm
awareness of others' actions
body awareness

Audience: toddler, preschool

Group Size: pair

Setting: transition, language, quiet
time together

Directions: *To Market, To Market*   This game allows you and a child to tune into each other's body movements while following the rhythm of the words in the chant. Place a child on your lap, face each other, and hold hands. In rhythm to the chant, bounce the child on your knees while saying the following nursery rhyme. During the last two lines, gently pull one of the child's arms forward, while pushing the other back (locomotive fashion). Then reverse this motion in rhythm with the chant.

> To market, to market, to buy a fat pig,
> Home again, home again, jiggity jig.
> To market, to market, to buy a fat hog,
> Home again, home again, jiggity jog.

Variations: 1. Substitute other animals' names for pig and hog and appropriate rhyming words for jig and jog, for example: *cow/bow* and *sheep/beep.*
2. *This Little Pig*   Hold or face the child. Start with the big toe and gently squeeze each toe while repeating the nursery rhyme. As you say *wee, wee, wee,* swiftly creep your fingers up to the child's tummy or chin and give a tickle. The youngster quickly learns to anticipate the tickle and greets it with great laughter!

> This little pig went to market.
> This little pig stayed home.
> This little pig had roast beef.
> This little pig had none.
> This little pig said, Wee, wee, wee!
> All the way home.

Chants and echoes

Develops: laughter
language
listening skills
rhythm
turn-taking
social interaction
positive self-image

Audience: toddler (E), preschool,
kindergarten, primary (V)

Group Size: pair or small group

Setting: language, dramatics (V-1), circle
time, transition, traveling, self-
awareness

Directions: Chanting is a natural activity for young children. They love to repeat and hear words over and over and enjoy the rhythm. To play with a small group, chant, *Who sees you?* The children respond, for example, *Mrs. Borden sees me*! This chant may be repeated as long as it is enjoyable. It can be changed to *Who (hears, likes, sings to, cooks lunch for) you?* To make the game special, have fun as a pair using specific names. For a playful activity, give a little tickle while chanting *Who tickles Alex?* The child giggles back, *Kevin tickles Alex!*

Easier: *Echo*   The youngest players will become delightfully silly as they imitate, or repeat again and again, a chant of: *Bye-bye! Bye-bye!, See you! See you!* or *Love you! Love you!* The chants may be loud-then-soft or fast-then-slow.

Variations: 1. Ask the children to dramatize various chants while reciting them. Help them establish a rhythm. *Clickety, clack. The train's on the track. Run! Run! Catch the sun!*
2. Encourage the players to make up their own chants about familiar activities or their friends; for example: *Jackie and Judy eat tutti-frutti. Yum, yum, yum!*

Adaptation: Echoes and chants lend themselves beautifully to language activities for bilingual children and those who are involved in speech therapy.

Jack-in-the-box

Develops: gross and fine (V) motor skills
listening skills
concepts of place and position
action-word coordination
anticipation
imagination

Audience: toddler, preschool, kindergarten, primary (H)

Group Size: pair, small or large group

Setting: movement, playground, gym, circle time, transition, language, dramatics

Directions: The children pretend to be a Jack (or Jill)-in-the Box. When you say *Jack in the box,* the players squat down, as if they were inside of a box. If you tell them, *Jack* out *of the box,* they quickly jump up out of the box. The youngsters must listen carefully in case you say a direction twice in a row. This is a great transition game that allows the youngsters to hop up and down on rainy days.

Harder: The children form a circle. Give various commands for the players to follow: *Jill jump in the circle, Jill step out of the circle, Jill skip around the circle, Jill walk backwards around the circle, Jill hold hands and come to the center of the circle,* or *Jill circle to the left.*

Variation: Instead of participating in an active transition game, a quiet fingerplay is sometimes appropriate. Young children love to watch with anticipation and delight as you flick Jack out of his box. Older students may join you in doing the fingerplay. Make a fist with the thumb facing upwards, then tuck it inside the fingers. After the second line, children shake their heads *Yes!* On this cue, the thumb pops up out of the fingers.

Jack-in-the-Box, sitting so still.
Won't you come out?
Yes, I will!

Let's go on a hunt!

Develops: listening skills
action-word coordination
awareness of others' actions
sequencing
gross motor skills
imagination

Audience: preschool, kindergarten, primary

Group Size: pair, small or large group

Setting: playground, dramatics,
circle time, language

Directions: A treasure hunt is a special way for children to practice following directions. It is also a wonderful means of moving to another activity or discovering a new learning center. The entire crew may solve the treasure hunt together or one pirate can follow a verbal treasure map. Give children simple clues, such as: *take three steps forward along the green floor tiles, turn around twice,* and *stamp your feet 4 times.* The treasure waiting at the end of the hunt could be a bonus trip to the playground or the uncovering of a new toy in the sandbox. Older children enjoy making up hints for their friends to follow.

Variation: *Lion Hunt* is a well-loved camp favorite. Every statement is accompanied by a motion; the players repeat both the words and actions. For example, as you say *let's walk,* slap hands on knees; after *let's run,* slap hands faster. Move arms in a swimming motion as you *cross the river.* To *cross the swamp,* point fingers and pull them up, make a *slurping* sound. *Climb through the grass* by pushing it apart; say *Swishhh!* Pretend to *climb a tree.* Continue pantomiming movements. Just before you reach the last line, quickly repeat all the motions and words, as if you're running back to where you started. At the end, calmly say the last line.

> Let's go on a lion hunt. Put on your coat. Your hat. Your boots. Now you're ready.
> Let's go! Open the door. Close it. Let's walk. Let's run!
> There's a river. We must cross it. There's a swamp. We must cross it.
> Tall grass ahead. We must go through it. Tall tree ahead. Let's climb it.
> I see a cave. Let's go in. I feel a tail. I feel a furry head.
> I see two eyes. I think it's a lion! Let's go home!
> Oh, it was just a kitty!

Popcorn! Crackerjacks!

Develops: gross motor skills
action-word coordination
transforming situations
impulse control
imagination
awareness of others' actions

Audience: toddler, preschool,
kindergarten, primary

Group Size: small or large group

Setting: movement, playground, gym,
dramatics, after snack, science

Directions: This game is particularly good to play after the class has popped corn and eaten it. The children crouch down pretending to be *popcorn kernels*. Turn on the heat under *the pan* (the floor). Slowly say *Pop, pop, pop!* with an irregular beat. The tiny kernels move sluggishly at first. Turn up the heat and repeat the pops louder and more frequently. The kernels begin to hop and jump higher in the pan. As they turn into popcorn, they join in making popping sounds. To end this activity, you may eat the kernels, who then sit down as soon as they have been devoured! To extend the game, pretend to pour syrup over the popcorn. The kernels pop next to each other, touch, and begin to stick together. Soon, little groups of caramel corn are hopping together. When the clusters bump into each other, the sticky masses eventually become one giant, jumping, popcorn ball! This is the world's best activity to release tension and get rid of excess energy. It always produces a wonderful case of the giggles!

Left! Right!

Develops: gross motor skills
concept of position
directionality
listening skills
awareness of others' actions
action-word coordination

Audience: primary

Group Size: large group

Setting: classroom at desks, playground, gym, movement, language

Directions: This game is guaranteed to discharge energy and provide lots of laughs for the players. Children also get a chance to review the concept of left and right. Have the youngsters sit at desks in rows or stand in the pattern of desks in rows. When you say *Move right!* the players go to the seat/position on their right. The last player in the row stands in the aisle. If you call *Move right!* again, two children will stand in the aisle. *Move left!* puts some players back in their seats.

Variation: Instead of standing in the aisle, the children without a seat run to the other side of the row to sit in a seat or stand in a position vacated by another.

Harder: In addition to commands of *Move right!* and *Move left!* you may also tell the players to *Move forward!* and *Move backwards!*

Variation: *The Wave*   Have children sit in a circle. One player vacates a spot and goes to the center. You rapidly call out, *Move left!* or *Move right!* The center child tries to spot a gap in the circle and runs to sit in the empty space as the players move like a giant wave following the commands. After everyone has moved to a space, the newly-seated child selects the next center player and the game begins again.

Statues

Develops: creative movement/
improvisation
body awareness
awareness of self in space
sequencing skills
listening skills
understanding of cues
impulse control

Audience: toddler, preschool, kindergarten,
primary

Group Size: pair, small or large group

Setting: playground, gym, music, dramatics,
movement

Directions: This game allows the children to move freely in space. It is a great activity when there is a case of the wiggles going around! Explain that you will hum a little song while the players dance up, down, and all around. When you stop humming, the players must stop dancing. They freeze and turn into statues in all sorts of unusual poses—legs apart, hands up in the air, or in a partial twist. If you don't wish to sing, simply say *Dance!* to begin and *Stop!* to turn the players into statues.

Easier: Pick up a child, hold him or her close in a dancing position and hum. Dance as a pair with dips and twirls. When you stop humming, you become a statue. Of course, hugging and giggling are allowed!!

Variation: Have pairs of children hold hands and dance together to the humming. When the music ends, they stop and become a large sculpture together. For another variation, see which pair can go the longest without laughing.

Adaptation: Pair a hearing-impaired youngster or a child in a wheelchair with a dancing partner.

Snow and sun fun

Develops: imagination
gross motor skills
awareness of self in space
sequencing skills
transforming situations
awareness of others' actions
concepts of shape (E,H)

Audience: toddler (E), preschool,
kindergarten, primary (H)

Group Size: individual (E), small (E) or large
group

Setting: playground, gym, beach or sandy
area (E,H), imaginative play,
movement, science, snow (E,H)

Directions: *Jack Frost and the Sun*
Choose several youngsters to be
Jack Frost and one to play *the
Sun.* The other children pretend
to take a trip and move around
the area by skipping, twirling,
hopping, or walking. Whomever
the Jack Frosts paint (touch) with
their magic brushes must freeze
in their positions. Then the Sun
quickly rushes to thaw out the
frozen children so they may
continue on their travels.

Easier: *Angels in the Snow/Sand*   This is an old favorite for children of all ages. It works
equally well in the snow or on a sunny day at the beach in dry sand. The *Angels* lie down on
their backs in the snow or sand, stretch out their arms and legs, and move them up and
down in big arcs. After the *Angels* stand up, they will see the imprints they have made.

Harder: *Fox and Geese*   Here is another game that can be played in the snow or sand. First
have the players stamp out a gigantic circle with six spokes and a hub in the center, which is
home base. One player is the *Fox* while the other participants are the *Geese.* The Fox
chases the Geese along the pathways. (The Geese, but not the Fox, may hop across from
one spoke to another.) Only one Goose at a time can use home base. If a second Goose
enters the hub, the first one must leave. A tagged Goose becomes the next Fox.

Change!

Develops: listening skills
sequencing skills
awareness of roles
gross motor skills
quick reactions
familiarity with simple melodies (E)

Audience: toddler, (SE), preschool (E), kindergarten, primary

Group Size: pair (SE) or large group

Setting: movement, playground, gym, music (E), circle time

Directions: *Squirrel in the Tree* Pairs of children hold hands to form a hollow *tree*. Inside each tree, a third child is a *squirrel*. One child is the extra squirrel. (If there are two extra children, the second assists you.) When you say *Change!* and clap your hands, the squirrels run for other trees. The extra squirrel also tries to find a home. If it is successful, the player left out becomes the new extra squirrel. Rotate squirrels and trees frequently to give everyone a chance to switch roles.

Easier: *Partners Change* Have children pair up, hold hands, and sing the following to the tune of *Mary Had a Little Lamb*. On the word *change*, the players find another partner. The song begins again. This time, players try a different form of movement (*dance, skip, jump*).

Partners *march* and move around,
March around, move around.
Partners *march* and move around
Until it's time to change!

Still Easier: For a cuddly game with a young child, hold the youngster while singing and performing the motions. On the word *change*, simply alter the movement.

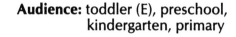

Blind man's buff

Develops: tactile sensitivity
body awareness
awareness of other players
decoding skills

Audience: toddler (E), preschool,
kindergarten, primary

Group Size: small (E) or large group

Setting: circle (indoor or outdoor)

Directions: Ask the child designated as the *blind person* to close his or her eyes. The other players form a moving circle with *It*, the blind child, in the center. When *It* claps his or her hands three times, the children in the circle must stop. *It* points to a child who must step into the circle. With the eyes still closed, the *blind person* feels this player's face and tries to guess who it is in three guesses. Giggling may give the player away! Then *It* and the player exchange places.

Easier: Have a small group sit on the floor. One child closes his or her eyes. You lead *It* by the hand to a group member. The *blind person* touches this youngster and attempts to guess his or her name. Simple hints may be given, for example: *her braids are brown.*

Harder: *Still Pond* should be played within a well-defined, small area free of obstacles. The players may move around until *It*, whose eyes are closed, says: *Still pond, no more moving. It* walks around until a stopped player is touched and must guess who this player is.

Variation: *Animal Blind Man's Buff*
It points to someone in the circle, then requests that this player make an animal sound, for example, a dog's bark. From this noise, *It* tries to guess the player.

Your number's up

Develops: concentration
patterning (V)
listening skills
number coding
alertness to sensory cues
awareness of others' actions

Audience: kindergarten (E), primary, older primary (V)

Group Size: small (E) or large group

Setting: at desks, circle time, math

Directions: *Seven Up* is a traditional game. Seven players are *It*. The rest of the children put their heads on their desks or in their laps and each holds up a fist with thumb extended. The seven players stealthily move about the room; each pushes down one child's thumb. The seven go to the front of the room and announce, *Seven up!* The youngsters whose thumbs were tapped stand up and try to guess who touched their thumbs. If they guess correctly, they exchange places. If a player is not guessed, he or she continues to be *It*. In this quiet, long-time favorite game, it is important to urge the participants to keep the activity moving quickly so that it does not drag.

Easier: 1. The child is allowed three guesses. 2. Play with a small group. Have two or three children serve as *It*.

Variation: *Concentration*   Give each child a number. When a player's number is called, this rhythmic pattern must be repeated: two slaps on the thighs, two claps of the hands, and then two stomps of the feet. The game originator names his or her number on the first foot stomp and announces another player's on the second stomp. This second player then claps the pattern and stomps his or her and another player's number. If a player misses, the play goes back to the last person whose number was up. It's easy and lots of fun when numbers are mixed up!

A silly race

Develops: sense of humor
gross motor skills
sequencing skills
team awareness
imagination
concepts of distance and speed
balance (V)

Audience: toddler (SE), preschool (E),
late kindergarten, primary

Group Size: small or large group

Setting: playground, gym, dramatics,
movement

Directions: Allow the children to form several teams with an equal number of players. If there are extra children, they may help as starters or judges who assist in declaring the fastest team. For a silly relay, the teams start at a designated line. The players race by running, hopping or skipping to a certain spot, think of something silly to do *(make a face, wiggle their hands like limp spaghetti)* and then race back to tag the next team member to run the silly relay. The first team to complete the race wins. The children relish the freedom to act silly!

Easier: Rainy days turn into fun days with this activity. Instead of having relay teams, request that on the word *Go!,* all of the youngsters run across the area and do something silly when they reach the other side. Then they run back.

Still Easier: Young children love to simply race across the room at the signal *Go!,* and tag or hop into the arms of a waiting adult. This is a great way to initiate laughter!

Variation: *Heel, Toe, and Away We Go!* Each player puts one foot forward and then places the heel of the other foot against the toe of that foot. The racers continue across the designated race area this way and then run back. This becomes a silly relay race! The children laugh a great deal as they waver back and forth trying to keep their balance!

Tricks

Develops: sense of humor
gross motor skills
cooperation
balance
timing
directionality
imagination

Audience: preschool, kindergarten (H,V),
primary (H,V)

Group Size: pairs

Setting: playground, gym, dramatics,
movement, circle time

Directions: *Wheelbarrow*   This is a great balancing trick; however, it is difficult to perform if the players are laughing! One child puts both hands on the floor. The other child stands between this player's legs and picks up his or her ankles. The wheelbarrow *walks* forward on its hands while the other child attempts to steer.

Harder: *Roll Out the Barrel*   After joining hands, two children put their arms up high over their heads and twist in the same direction. Have the pairs try to twist several times in a row. It's fun!

Variation: *Leap Frogs*   Have children form pairs. One child is the *Frog* and the other child squats very low to the floor to play the *Lily Pad.* The Frog places his or her hands on the Lily Pad's back. Legs apart, the Frog leaps over the Pad. The pair reverse roles, trying not to fall in, as they leap across their *pond.*

Many of the activities in this chapter lend themselves to indoor and outdoor play. Through movement, the children are able to freely explore their own bodies, the space around them, and various means of locomotion. While experimenting with creative movement, the young players turn into exciting people, animals, and objects—real and imaginary. And what better way to assist children in ridding themselves of pent-up steam in a positive way! Gross motor coordination skills are enhanced through practice in a game-like atmosphere.

Bubbles

Develops: creative movement
awareness of self in space
cooperation
awareness of others' actions
concepts of cause and effect
imagination
concept of shape

Audience: preschool, kindergarten, primary

Group Size: individual, pair (H), small (V) or
large group (V)

Setting: circle time, movement,
playground, gym, dramatics,
science, self-awareness

Directions: This game makes the players aware of the space surrounding them. First, the children gently *blow* a bubble all around themselves to create their bubble space. It may be as big or as little as they wish. The children must move very carefully so that the bubbles don't pop. This is an excellent activity to separate youngsters before they begin a project that requires elbow room. Bubble spaces have a wonderful, soothing effect on the children!

Harder: Two players hold hands to form a bubble. Its takes cooperation and coordination to move together from one place to the next, to twirl and float through the air without hitting another bubble pair and popping!

Variation: All of the children join hands to form a giant bubble circle. Give the huge bubble specific directions such as: *float to the left, twirl to the door, swirl down low,* or *dance on top of the water.* The players must coordinate their motions.

Turtle peek

Develops: body awareness
sensitivity to stimulation
visual discrimination
focusing
gross motor skills
creative movement
imagination

Audience: toddler, preschool

Group Size: pair (adult and child) or
very small group

Setting: lap or floor, playground,
circle time, movement

Directions: Have several children lie on the floor on their stomachs with their arms and legs tucked under their *shells*. Gently pull up their heads and move them side to side in order for the *turtles* to peek around. To increase visual discrimination, ask the turtles to focus on objects in their proximity. For example, ask: *Can you peek and see the chair?* Tug lightly on the turtles' legs and arms to unfold them from their shells. If any children need extra stimulation or special attention, softly stroke their limbs. Allow the emerging turtles to practice their crawling skills around the room. For close contact with the very young, hold a child in your lap. This child tucks arms and legs under his or her shell. You gently work through the above movements.

Harder: Keeping their heads up and eyes open, have the turtles crawl through an obstacle course: under a table, around a chair or over a hollow block, and so on.

Variations: Have the children try other animal movements, such as an *elephant roll*. Ask the children to lie on the floor. Put your hands together to form a trunk and gently push the children in order to roll them over and over. For a silly laughing game, make loud elephant trumpets as the children are rolled with the trunk.

Adaptation: Assist the physically challenged child with patterning through play by manipulating the child's extremities. This game provides an opportunity for close, warm, physical contact for the youngster who needs special nurturing.

Pair play

Develops: gross motor skills
cooperation
sequencing skills
timing
problem-solving
physical strength

Audience: preschool (E),
kindergarten, primary

Group Size: pairs, large group (V)

Setting: movement, gym, dramatics (E)

Directions: *Pair Pull-ups* Two children sit on the floor across from each other with knees bent and feet flat. Holding hands and pulling together, they try to stand up and then sit back down again.

Easier: *Rowboat* While singing *Row, Row, Row Your Boat*, two players sit on the floor facing each other. They spread their legs apart with feet touching. The pair hold hands and rock back and forth as if rowing.

Harder: *Chinese Get-up and Go* A pair of children sit back to back. They hook elbows and bend their knees with feet flat on the floor. The two push their backs together and try to wiggle up to a standing position. For an added challenge, have them try to sit back down again.

Variation: *Back to Back* This is a group game. The children play in pairs. One extra child plays *It*. The pairs stand back to back with arms linked. When *It* yells *Change!*, all of the players run to find a new partner. If *It* hooks arms with a partner, the child left without a partner becomes the next *It*.

Walk a while

Develops: gross motor skills
action-word coordination
imagination

Audience: toddler (E), preschool,
kindergarten, primary

Group Size: pair, small or large group

Setting: classroom, movement, transition,
gym, outdoors

Directions: This is an excellent activity when the children have been sitting awhile. Allow the children to loosen up by walking around the room in various ways. Ask the group to walk as *heavily as possible, like dinosaurs!* Then, ask that they *walk lightly, pretending to be kittens* or *trying to walk on eggs.* Have them *walk with special emotions: happily, angrily,* or *fearfully;* or *as if they are stuck in the mud* or *their feet have turned to gelatin.* Say *Freeze!* when the children should stop walking.

Easier: Before assigning a specific walk, demonstrate it first for the children to imitate.

Harder: *Partner Walks*   The youngsters select partners for walks. Have them walk forward together, side by side, and follow each other. Exchange leadership roles. Have the pairs walk together using the same arm and leg movements—a real challenge!

Variation: *Walk Like the Animals*   Ask the players to walk: *as slowly as a turtle, as swiftly as a deer, as ploddingly as an elephant, on all fours like a cat,* or *as sprightly as a grasshopper.*

Adaptation: During *Partner Walks,* pair a child with poor coordination skills with a student who has excellent motor skills. Have them hold hands as they walk next to each other. This way the poorly-coordinated child feels the partner's natural rhythm.

Walk and talk like the animals

Develops: gross motor skills
imagination
action-word coordination
classification skills
body awareness
imitation of sounds

Audience: toddler (E), preschool, kindergarten, primary (H)

Group Size: pair, small or large group

Setting: playground, gym, dramatics, circle time, transition, movement, language

Directions: This is a fabulous game to release pent-up energy. Discuss with the children the many ways that animals move: *walk, run, hop, crawl, slither, waddle, swim* or *fly.* Have them demonstrate an animal movement of their choice, for example: *hop by squatting and leaping high in the air to imitate a frog.* For a real challenge, talk like the animal while walking like it. A frog might add a *chug-a-rum* to the hop! Allow all of the players to follow a leader's movements.

Easier: Name a specific animal which the children are familiar with, for instance, *a dog.* Demonstrate how the animal walks, exaggerating the motions if necessary. Give the players practice time, then have them imitate the appropriate sound, *woof, woof.*

Harder: After suggesting a particular motion, for example, *slither,* have the players name and demonstrate many animals that move that way. Have them add their specific sound if pertinent: snake—*ssss,* alligator—*hiss,* lizard—*sllllll,* and so on. The children will enjoy describing the sounds.

Variation: Tell a story during which the children act out animals' motions and voices. *The farmer called his horse* (children gallop and make neighing sounds) *to come to the chicken house* (children run with arms flapping at sides saying peep, peep). *The dog came, too* (children run on hands and knees and bark).

Adaptation: Many of these walks enable a group of children to practice exercises with the physically challenged child.

Animal walks

Develops: gross motor skills
classification skills
imagination
physical strength
balance
body awareness

Audience: late toddler (E), preschool (E),
kindergarten (E,H), primary (H)

Group Size: individual, small or large group

Setting: movement, dramatics, playground,
gym, transition

Directions: Besides enhancing gross motor skills, these animal walks are fun to do when moving from one activity to another. Depending upon the children's abilities, walks can be used for a team relay race or as an individual race. In a relay race, the players perform the specified motion while racing across the area and back to tag the next team racer.

Easier: *Crocodile Crawl*   For this game, the players lie on their tummies, elbows bent, and toes pointed out, as they crawl along.
Cat Walk   The players walk softly like kitties with hands on the floor and arms and legs bent slightly.
Elephant Lumber   The children hold their hands together to form trunks. They bend forward and swing their trunks as they walk with their legs straight.

Harder: *Duck Waddle*   The players squat down and grasp their ankles with their hands. They proceed to waddle along, one foot after the next.
Leap Frog   Knees are bent and hands touch the floor between them. To leap, the youngsters place their hands a bit in front of them, move their feet up to their hands, and croak *Ribbit, ribbit!*
Crab Walk   The players squat down and reach back. Then, they place both hands on the floor behind them without sitting. Crabs try walking backwards, sideways, or forward. If this is too difficult, allow the children to put their bottoms on the floor.

Adaptation: This game allows the physically challenged child to exercise certain body parts by practicing repetitive movements in an enjoyable way. *The crab walk* can be done with the entire class as a unique way to go to the cubbies and strengthen certain muscles.

Rhythms and rhymes

Develops: gross motor skills
rhythm
creative thinking
positive self-image
individuality
listening skills
language

Audience: preschool, kindergarten, primary

Group Size: pair, small or large group

Setting: gym, movement, dramatics,
circle time, language

Directions: Names have a natural rhythm. *E-lis-a-beth, E-lis-a-beth* is a fabulous name pattern to which the children can skip. *To-mas, To-mas* said rapidly and sharply is a wonderful medley that lends itself to running. *Sue-Sue-Sue* repeated slowly is a great walking rhythm. The joining of first and last names allows for a magnificent combination of rhythmic locomotion. Use a tip-toe-hop-hop-hop sequence to *Dar-yl-Straw-ber-ry, Dar-yl-Straw-ber-ry* . It is very exciting for each child to move to his or her own name.

Harder: Ask the players to think up movements to the rhythm of words in different categories, for example, food: *pea-nut-but-ter; march-march-march-march.*

Variation: You or the youngsters make up movement rhymes about their names. The group repeats each rhyme several times while performing the suggestion along with the selected child. *Sandi, Sandi twirls so handy; Pete, Pete, your feet stamp a beat; Nancy-Jo, Nancy-Jo, look how fast your feet can go!* Being on center stage for his or her personal rhyme enhances the self-image of any child!

Adaptation: Pair a child with poor motor skills with a well-coordinated youngster. When they hold hands for the activities, the child who needs assistance can feel the other's natural rhythm.

Similes

Develops: imagination
creative movement
language
thinking skills
ability to characterize
movement in space

Audience: toddler (E), kindergarten, primary

Group Size: pair, small or large group

Setting: movement, language, gym,
dramatics, circle time

Directions: Allow the children plenty of space and time to experiment as they dramatize various similes. Ask them to: *hop like a bunny in a cabbage patch, fly like a bird in a strong wind, sizzle like an egg frying in a hot pan,* or *slither like a snake in tall, wet grass.*

Easier: Simple similes for the youngsters to demonstrate may include: *swim like a fish, sleep like a baby, spin like a top, and fly like a kite.*

Variation: Encourage the players to create their own similes by thinking of ways to complete phrases such as these: *crawl like a _____, walk like a _____, leap like a _____, or stretch like a _____.* To extend the game, ask them to act out their suggestions.

Follow the leader

Develops: awareness of self in space
visual-motor skills
body awareness
directionality
awareness of others

Audience: toddler (E), preschool,
kindergarten, primary (H)

Group Size: pair, small or large group

Setting: playground, gym, classroom,
transition, movement exploration

Directions: Have the children line up, one behind the other. The first person in line is the leader. As the leader walks around the room, the players follow him or her and copy everything that he or she does. Some suggested movements for the leader may include: *raising arms in the air, hopping on one foot, skipping, crawling under a table.* To make the game more difficult, change the actions rapidly. This is a practical game to move the children together quickly from one place to another: to their cubbies to get their coats or to the block area to clean up.

Easier: Utilize these rhymes. Face the children, demonstrate and say, for example:

I clap my hands—one, two, three.
Now you do it just like me!
I stamp my feet--one, two.
See if you can do it, too!

Harder: *Mirror Game* Have the players work in pairs. The partners face each other. The leader changes facial expressions *(raises eyebrows, wiggles the nose)* or movement of body parts *(bends elbows).* The partner, the mirror image, must follow the leader. Be sure to have the partners switch roles.

Variation: Play with a partner. Move all around the room. Take turns being the leader. This is a great rainy day game!

Adaptation: Pair the visually-impaired child with a partner who whispers the changes to follow.

The bear went over the mountain

Develops: gross motor skills
action-word coordination
skill using prepositions
directionality
familiarity with simple melodies
listening skills
imagination

Audience: toddler (E), preschool,
kindergarten, primary

Group Size: pair or small group

Setting: classroom, playground, music,
dramatics, transition, language,
movement

Directions: Use the entire playground as the *Mountain.* The children are young bears who follow-the-leader: *over the mountain* (jungle gym), *up and down the mountain* (slide), *through the mountain* (sewer pipe tunnel) or *around the mountain,* (merry-go-around or walk around the sandbox). This game can also be played in the classroom by crawling under a table or walking around chairs, or as a means of transporting the children to their cubbies or the door. While acting out the verse, the bear cubs and you sing the popular song, *The Bear Went Over the Mountain,* substituting the desired prepositions. Another option is to have two players hold hands, London Bridge style, to represent the mountain. The bears go *through* or *around* them.

The bear went _____ the mountain.
The bear went _____ the mountain.
The bear went _____ the mountain.
To see what he could see.

Variation: After the last line, *To see what he could see*, the players use their imaginations to guess real *(trees, a river)* or silly views *(a hot fudge sundae).*

Easier: When you sing *up and over the mountain*, move a small child up high. Then swoop down together, as you sing *down the mountain.*

Simon says

Develops: gross motor skills
visual discrimination
listening skills
impulse control
body awareness
action-word coordination

Audience: toddler (E), preschool, kindergarten, primary

Group Size: pair, small or large group

Setting: movement, transition, circle time, language

Directions: The leader calls out a phrase, *Simon says do this!*, coordinated with a specific body action, for example: *touch the head, pat both shoulders.* The players who are standing repeat the motion. If the leader states *Do this,* eliminating the phrase *Simon says,* the players do not duplicate the motion. Those who do must sit down until the leader catches another player who doesn't wait for *Simon says.* The children quickly become good listeners in this fast-paced game.

Easier: No tricks involved in this version! Say *Simon says do this!* and then make a simple motion, *a hop* or *touch a knee.* The players follow the action.

Variations: Have fun as you and your children make up your own versions of *Simon says!* Here are a few examples.
1. *Simon says touch (various parts of your body).*
2. *Simon says to move your body in different ways* (jump, kick, clap).
3. *Simon says to move your fingers (*three up, thumbs down, wiggle ten). This is a great version to play while sitting at desks or traveling.
4. *Simon says to move on words that begin or end with a specific letter.* For example, children move on *words that end with P—hop, jump, top, lap;* or, *move on words that begin with T—top, tub, time.*
5. *Have each child draw an imaginary clock around himself or herself. Then say, for example, Simon says to jump to six o'clock.* The child then hops toward the small hand position in the six o'clock spot.
6. *Simon says to jump up and down for things in a specific category, e.g., transportation* (boats, planes, bikes) or *food* (peas, bread, ice cream).
7. *Simon says to wave your arms for things that are round* (balloons, faces, potato chips) or *soft* (teddy bears, pillows, bunnies).

Mother may I?

Develops: gross motor skills
sequencing skills
action-word coordination
listening skills
social skills
thoughtfulness
turn-taking
vocabulary
imagination

Audience: toddler (E), preschool (E), kindergarten, primary

Group Size: small or medium group

Setting: classroom, gym, playground, dramatics, language, movement

Directions: Assign one player to be the mother. The other players stand approximately 25 feet away in a line facing Mother. Mother calls out to a player, for example: *Derek, you may take three giant steps.* He responds, *Mother, may I?* She says *Yes!* and he then takes three giant steps. Mother then continues the game by calling out to other players. Vary the game by including the following steps: *baby* (tiny ones), *umbrella* (twirling ones), *crab* (on all fours), *hops*, or *leaps*. If a player forgets to say *Mother, may I?*, he or she must go back to the starting place. When a child is close enough to touch Mother, he or she becomes the new mother and the game begins again. This traditional game encourages the players to interact politely with each other. The children may add to the game by responding with well-mannered words and phrases, such as *please, thank you,* and *you're welcome.*

Easier: Mother utilizes only one or two different types of steps. You may also call the game, *Giant Steps,* and eliminate the use of *Mother, may I?* No child would therefore have to be sent back to the beginning of the line.

Harder: Encourage the children to create many unusual steps—*bunny hops, football punts, or ballerina whirls.*

Adaptation: Have the physically challenged child work with a partner.

Me and my shadow

Develops: movement exploration
problem-solving
awareness of self in space
gross motor skills
directionality
action-word coordination
verbal understanding

Audience: toddler, preschool, kindergarten, primary (V)

Group Size: individual, pair, small or large group

Setting: outdoors, playground

Directions: Go outside on a sunny day; have the children locate their shadows. Encourage them to experiment with moving their shadows various ways by moving their bodies. Can they make their shadows taller, shorter, wider, narrower? Can children run faster than their shadows? Can they make the shadows move backwards?

Variations: 1. *Shadow Tag* Ask each child to select a partner. The two take turns attempting to step on each other's shadows. The players may try various forms of locomotion: *walking, running,* or *skipping.* (Or play this as a group game. One child is *It* and steps on the others' shadows.)
2. Call out a specific body part and request that the shadow perform a certain task, for example: *wiggle your leg, wave your arms,* or *shake your head.*

Harder: Have the shadow move a combination of features *(right hand waves while the left leg stamps)* or perform particular actions *(swimming, dancing, climbing,* and so on).

Adaptations: After reading the leader's lips for shadow commands, the hearing-impaired child has the added advantage of observing the body and shadow movements of others, as visual checks, while participating in the activity. Allow the physically challenged child to work with another child. The two discuss shadow motions and take turns acting out appropriate positions.

Leaping lions

Develops: gross motor skills
ability to comprehend
instructions
practice to extend growth
concepts of space, distance, and
speed

Audience: toddler (E), preschool,
kindergarten, primary

Group Size: pair (E), small or large group

Setting: playground, gym, classroom,
dramatics, circle time, transition,
movement

Directions: Give the players lots of opportunities to discover different ways to leap or jump. Depending upon their abilities, ask them to demonstrate a variety of ways, or make the following suggestions for them: *to leap from two feet to two feet; from two feet to one foot; from one foot to two feet; from one foot to one foot;* and *in different directions: down, up, with a turn, in place,* or *running.* As the children practice, they may try combinations—*run, leap, hop,* and *walk.*

Easier: Young children love to leap into an adult's waiting arms. Little leapers may jump from a bouncing board, set of steps, or platform. Caution them not to leap, however, until you say, *Ready!* End the leaps with hugs and laughs!

Variations: Have the children *leap like lions,* then dramatize the movements of other leaping animals, for example: *deer, panthers,* and *rabbits.* Continue exploring the movement of different animals. Ask the children to demonstrate how: *horses gallop, snakes slither, fish swim,* and so on.

All made of hinges

Develops: fine and gross motor skills
ability to comprehend
instructions
action-word coordination
awareness of self in space

Audience: toddler (E), preschool,
kindergarten, primary

Group Size: pair, small or large group

Setting: indoors, outdoors, circle time,
gym, transition, movement

Directions: The players spread out in order to have space to bend. The children may sit, lie on the floor, stand, or play while sitting at their desks. You begin by saying, *I'm all made of hinges from my head to my ends.* The youngsters then bend as many body parts as they wish in order to warm up. You then repeat the above line inserting specific body-part hinges, for example: *from my fingers to my elbows* or *from my toes to my hips.* After offering several specific directions, interject, *I'm all made of hinges from my head to my ends.* This command, once again, allows the players to bend all parts freely. This game is a nice diversion and gives the children an opportunity to relax.

Easier: Demonstrate simple suggestions for the players to follow.

Harder: Have the children act out two commands at the same time.

Variations: Move the body hinges at different speeds: *very slowly, rapidly,* or *fast-then-slow.*
Work in pairs. Have one child move another player's body hinges.

Adaptation: This is an excellent game for the physically challenged child to practice moving specific body parts.

Tag

Develops: gross motor skills
awareness of self in space
awareness of others' actions
sequencing skills
game strategy

Audience: toddler (E), preschool,
kindergarten, primary

Group Size: pair (E), small or large group

Setting: playground, gym, movement

Directions: An old-fashioned game, tag is played by children in many countries. The player designated as *It* runs after the others. When *It* tags someone, he or she becomes the new *It*. Little children simply love the thrill of the chase!

Easier: *Partner Tag*   Have children work in pairs; one child in a pair is *It* and chases the other. When he or she is tagged, that person becomes the new *It*. For another version that's fun, you are *It*. Whenever you catch a young child, scoop him or her up and give a squeeze and a hug for a very special shared moment!

Variations: *Squat Tag*   The player who is being chased squats to avoid being tagged.
Japanese Tag   The runner places one hand on the spot where tagged. He or she becomes the new *It* and tries to tag the others with the hand that's free.
Couple Tag   Holding hands, two players chase the rest. When a player is tagged, he or she forms the couple, with the first *It* of the pair breaking away to join the other players.
Swim Tag   The players are Fish swimming in the ocean. One child is the Fisherman who tries to catch the Fish. An area is designated as the *coral reef* or *home base (a wall or jungle gym)*. When the Fish touch it, they cannot be caught. However, when the fisherman says *Swim!*, all of the players must leave the base.

Natural enemies

Develops: gross motor skills
listening skills
game strategy
awareness of others' actions
impulse control
imagination

Audience: preschool (E), kindergarten,
primary (H)

Group Size: pair, small (E) or large
group (H,V)

Setting: movement, dramatics, science,
circle time

Directions: *Cat and Dog*   Most animals have natural enemies, and usually, one tries to chase the other out of its territory. The following chase games involve cats and their natural enemies, dogs and mice. This game involves two children. One child is the *Cat;* the other is the *Dog.* The players close their eyes and place a hand on a large table (without sharp corners). Keeping eyes closed, the Cat *meows,* the Dog *barks.* The Dog chases the Cat around the table, trying to locate it by listening for the sounds it makes. (The Cat anticipates the location of the Dog by listening for its barks.) The Dog and Cat may turn and race around the table in either direction. If the children tire in this intense game, allow them to rest.

Easier: *Angry Cat*   The child designated as the *Dog* approaches various *Cats* and *barks.* The Cats, on their hands and knees, arch their backs, make an angry hissing sound and then run away. The Dog chases them and tags one, who becomes the next Dog!

Harder: *Cat and Mouse*   The players hold hands in a circle. The child who is the *Cat* begins on the outside; the child who is the *Mouse* is inside. The players raise and lower their arms to let the Mouse in and out of the mouse holes. They try to keep the Cat from catching the Mouse by blocking it with lowered arms. When the Mouse is captured, or after a two-minute limit, two other children play the Cat and Mouse.

Variation: *Cat and Mice*   The *Cat* hides under a table or under the teacher's desk. Several *Mice* creep up and make squeaking noises. The Cat wakes up, meows, and chases the Mice, who try to run back to their holes (seats) without being tagged. If a Mouse is caught, it becomes the Cat. Otherwise, you pick a new Cat.

Adaptation: These are appropriate games to play if a child has been excluded or chased away by peers. Discuss ways that the animals and children can live and play together.

Ring around the rosie

Develops: gross motor skills
sequencing skills
familiarity with simple melodies
group consciousness
listening skills
the concept of speed (V)

Directions: This is usually the child's first group game and is an early favorite among parents and children. The children hold hands, form a circle, and walk in the same direction, as they sing the following verses. On the word *down,* the youngsters squat down, usually accompanied by much laughter.

> Ring around the rosie
> A pocket full of posies.
> Ashes, ashes,
> We all fall down.

Adaptation: If someone needs special nurturing, pick up the child and hold him or her close while dancing and singing. Swoop down together.

Audience: toddler, preschool, kindergarten

Group Size: pair or small group

Setting: playground, gym, classroom, music, movement

Variations: 1. Children enjoy creating their own silly versions, like *falling up* (jumping high in the air) instead of down or *running* instead of walking.
2. *Motor Boat* While holding hands and walking in a circle, the players chant the following verses. They gather speed as they recite the verses, through *Rhmmmm!* then gradually slow down. At the last line, *Out of gas!,* they come to a stop, then sit on the floor.

> Motor boat, motor boat, go so slow
> Motor boat, motor boat, go so fast.
> Motor boat, motor boat, step on the gas.
> Rhmmmm!
> Motor boat, motor boat, go so slow,
> Chug, chug,
> Out of gas!

Charley over the water

Develops: gross motor skills
impulse control
listening skills
awareness of role reversals
rhythm
sequencing skills

Directions: Gather the youngsters together and form a circle by joining hands. If the group is small, one child in the center becomes *Charley*. With a large group, allow several children into the center at one time in order to give as many youngsters as possible a turn. Holding hands, the players walk around *Charley* chanting the verses. *Charley* extends his or her arms and points a finger throughout the chant. On the word *me*, the circling children stop. The person *Charley* points to, switches places with *Charley*. He or she goes into the center and the game begins again.

Audience: preschool, kindergarten, primary

Group Size: small or large group

Setting: playground, gym, classroom, music, movement

Harder: On the word *me*, the child who is *Charley* attempts to tag one of the players holding hands in the circle. The tagged child becomes *Charley*. In order to be *safe*, the players try to squat down and touch the ground before they are tagged.

Variation: Try different movements by having children *run* or *skip*.

Charley over the water.
Charley over the sea.
Charley caught a big fish,
But can't catch me!

Shake up

Develops: gross motor skills
body awareness
understanding of words
impulse control
awareness of self in space

Audience: toddler, preschool, kindergarten, primary

Group Size: small or large group

Setting: indoors, outdoors, circle time, movement, self-awareness, music

Directions: In the beginning, point to a specific child sitting in the circle and call out his or her name. This child stands in the center of the circle. Everyone chants the song using that child's name. When the children chant *shake up*, the standing child jiggles all over until he or she hears, *that's enough*. The child sits down and points to another. The game is then repeated. If group participation is desired, all of the children shake their bodies and hands when they hear the phrase *shake up*. This is a marvelous energy releaser!

Here comes Lila going to town.
Here comes Lila fooling around.
Now Lila, shake up, shake up,
Shake up, shake up!
That's enough! Sit down!

Variation: 1. The leader describes a motion that the selected child acts out. Some suggested motions include: *turn around, jump up,* and *dance fast.*
2. To involve more children, play with two youngsters in the center. If they wish, they dance as a pair.
3. To keep the children on their toes, periodically interject, *Here comes everyone going to town.* In this case, all of the players must stand up and wiggle!

Arms up!

Develops: gross motor skills
  turn-taking
  listening skills
  familiarity with simple melodies
  awareness of roles
  sequencing skills

Directions: *A-Hunting We Will Go*   The players form a circle, hold hands and walk to the right. While the *Fox* skips around the outside of the circle in the opposite direction, the players chant or sing the following verses to the tune of *The Noble Duke of York.* As they sing the third line, the players raise their arms up high to allow the Fox into the circle, then lower them to trap the Fox. As they sing, *And then we'll let him go,* the children raise their arms in an arch to let the Fox escape. At the end of the song, the Fox quickly selects another to take his or her place.

  Oh, a-hunting we will go.
  A-hunting we will go.
  We'll catch a little fox
  And put it in a box
  And then we'll let it go!

Harder: *Birds and Scarecrow*   One child is selected to play the *Scarecrow;* three or four play the *Birds.* The rest of the children form a large circle and hold hands. The Scarecrow is in the center of the circle protecting the garden. Three or four Birds fly around outside of the circle. The circle players raise and lower their arms in an arch to allow the Birds to fly in and out of the garden to eat. The Scarecrow, who must remain in the garden, tries to catch (tag) the Birds. As soon as a Bird is caught, he or she also becomes a Scarecrow. When the Birds are all caught, a new Scarecrow and Birds are chosen, and the game begins again.

Audience: late toddler (V), preschool (V), kindergarten, primary (H)

Group Size: large group

Setting: movement, music, circle time, playground, gym

Variation: *London Bridge*   This traditional and simple game is ever-popular. Two children form an arch with their hands high in the air. The other players form a line and walk in a circle, passing under the bridge while singing the verses. On the last phrase, the bridge collapses and the player passing through is captured. This player then replaces half of the bridge.

  London bridge is falling down,
  Falling down, falling down.
  London bridge is falling down,
  My fair lady.

Moving day

Develops: gross motor skills
listening skills
group consciousness
sequencing skills
awareness of role reversals
quick reactions

Audience: kindergarten (V), primary

Group Size: large group

Setting: gym, classroom, movement,
social studies

Directions: The players sit in a circle. An *It* is chosen, sits in the center and asks a specific player, *Is your neighbor moving?* If this player says *no, It* questions another player by asking, *Is your neighbor moving?* If this player replies *yes,* he or she then states that the neighbor on the *right* (or *left*) is moving to another child's house. The two children mentioned must quickly stand up and run to exchange houses. At the same time, *It* also stands and runs to occupy a house. The person left without a home becomes the new *It.*

Variation: Pairs of children join hands to create houses, London Bridge style. (The houses are scattered around the room.) A third player lives in each house. An extra player does not have a home and wishes to move. Clap your hands three times to signal to the occupants of the houses to move to a new house. The single player quickly tries to find an unoccupied house. After several plays, the resident changes places with one of the walls of the house, giving another child a chance to move.

Fruit basket

Develops: gross motor skills
listening skills
classification skills
group consciousness
sequencing skills
quick reactions
awareness of role reversals

Audience: kindergarten (E,V), primary

Group Size: large group

Setting: playground, gym, classroom,
science, movement, after snack
preparation (V)

Directions: The children stand in a circle. One child goes into the center. Each person takes a turn and announces the name of a different fruit that he or she represents. The child in the center calls the names of two different fruits. These two players immediately run to change places while the center person tries to take one of their places. The player without a spot becomes the new center person. Periodically, the center player yells, *Fruit basket upset!*, then all of the players scramble for a new place. This gives the center player an excellent opportunity to locate a spot in the circle.

Easier: Give the players the names of only three or four fruits. If the center person calls out *peaches!* all of the peaches must exchange places while the center child tries to take one of their places.

Variation: *Salad Bowl* Play the game the same way as the easier version of Fruit Basket. This time substitute *salad vegetables.* To allow everyone to change places, the center child yells, *Salad toss!* This is a nice game to play after the children have prepared a salad for lunch or a snack.

LOOK OUT!

These visual awareness games encourage children to look carefully at the world around them and to investigate their surroundings. Through play, youngsters sharpen their observational skills by noting details, features, characters' roles, and actions. While applying their visual memories, children strengthen concentration. They learn to recognize and compare colors, shapes, and body parts as they play these visual discrimination games.

On a walk

Develops: color discrimination
memory
language
creative dramatics (V)

Audience: preschool, kindergarten, primary

Group Size: pair or small group(s)

Setting: walk, playground, dramatics (V), traveling, science, language

Directions: *Rainbow Walk*   Before taking a walk, assign the children a specific color, for example: *green*. Ask them to point to an item of that color as soon as they see it—*leaves, grass, a pine tree*. After returning from the walk, have the children try to remember all of the things of that color they have seen. For a real challenge, give each child, or each pair, different colors to look for, then talk about. This game can also be played with shapes.

Variations: *Do You See What I Saw?* As a means of review, a player thinks of something special that he or she saw on the walk and dramatizes it. After watching, the other players guess what the actor or actress saw. Be sure everyone has an opportunity to act out what was observed. *Window Shopping*   While on a walk, request that the players look carefully at the *objects in a store window*. Then, have them close their eyes. Each child takes a turn naming as many items as possible. Afterwards, they open their eyes to check the objects. Vary this game by observing a *garden patch, section of a beach, pond life* or *a park playground*.

Match me

Develops: gross motor skills
body awareness
ability to match visual stimuli
memory

Audience: toddler (E), preschool,
kindergarten, primary

Group Size: pair, small or large group

Setting: indoors, outdoors, movement,
standing in a circle or line,
transition

Directions: At first, ask the children to match your body position. Change position. Ask the children to match the new position. When the group is able to do this comfortably, select a child to be the leader. While the others close their eyes, the leader changes his or her position. The leader says, *match me*, the players open their eyes and try to figure out the leader's change in position and match it. (Hints may be given.)

Easier: The leader's position changes are quite exaggerated, for example: *an arm raised high over the head.*

Harder: The leader's new positions are subtle, like *a finger moved* or *a change in facial expression.*

Variations: 1. The leader calls out *Match me!*, but this time changes two positions.
2. The leader changes a position and adds a motion, for example: he or she *raises an arm and waves it.*

Adaptation: Pair the physically challenged child with a friend. They discuss the body changes and take turns acting out positions that are appropriate.

LOOK OUT!

See and do

Develops: visual awareness
gross motor skills
imagination
awareness of others' actions
thinking skills
awareness of self

Audience: toddler, preschool,
kindergarten, primary

Group Size: small or large group

Setting: circle time, dramatics, language,
movement, self-awareness

Directions: These are popular games in which one child stands in the circle, thinks of an action, and then performs it for the others to follow. These three rhythmic games have simple repeating lines for the players or adult to chant or sing.

Little White Daisies   Insert a child's name while you sing the first section. As the second stanza is sung, the child performs an action, and the others imitate it.

> John is his first name,
> His first name, his first name.
> John is his first name,
> Among the little white daisies.
> This is what he likes to do,
> Likes to do, likes to do.
> This is what he likes to do,
> Among the little white daisies.

Monkey See and Monkey Do   The child in the center demonstrates an action; the group imitates it when the second line is sung. The children love hamming up their imitations as they pretend to be the copycat monkeys. For example:

> When I clap, clap, clap my hands,
> The monkeys clap, clap, clap their hands.
> Monkeys see and monkeys do,
> Monkeys do the same as you!

Our Favorite Things   Select one child to think of an activity; the rest participate and sing. Use favorite songs; just change the words, as the children circle around and sing along:
(tune: *The Mulberry Bush)*
> Now we'll do our favorite things,
> Our favorite things, our favorite things.
> Now we'll do our favorite things;
> We'll do them all together.
> This is the way we eat our pizza,
> Eat our pizza, eat our pizza.
> This is the way we eat our pizza;
> We'll do it all together.

Did you ever see a lassie?

Develops: visual discrimination
gross motor skills
imagination
awareness of others' actions
familiarity with simple melodies
thinking skills

Audience: preschool, kindergarten (V),
primary (H)

Group Size: large group

Setting: circle time, music, playground,
gym, dramatics, movement

Directions: *Did You Ever See a Lassie or Laddie?* The *Lassie* or *Laddie* stands in the center of the circle in this classic game. The players walk around the center child while singing the verses. During the second line, the Lassie or Laddie does something, such as *jumps* or *dances.* In the third line, the players stop and copy the action. At the last line, the Lassie or Laddie points to another child to be the next performer.

Did you ever see a lassie,
A lassie, a lassie?
Did you ever see a lassie
Go this way and that?
Go this way and that way.
Go this way and that way.
Did you ever see a lassie
Go this way and that?

Variation: The center child takes on the role of a particular character and dramatizes an appropriate action. Some suggestions may include: *a bunny, hop; Raggedy Andy, walk like a rag doll;* or, *a carpenter, hammer nails.* The players sing the song, replacing the word Lassie with the character's name, and imitate the actions.

Harder: The players suggest a character for the center child to pantomime.

Adaptation: To assist the visually impaired player, as soon as the Lassie or Laddie has performed the action after singing the first *Go this way*, the players name the motion. The child then acts out the movement, based on these cues.

Who's got the motion?

Develops: visual awareness
gross and fine motor skills
awareness of other players
collaboration

Audience: kindergarten, primary

Group Size: large group

Setting: circle time, movement

Directions: Ask the youngsters to sit in a circle. One child goes to the center of the circle and closes his or her eyes while you point to a leader. All of the players *clap their hands.* The leader changes the clapping to *patting the stomach, tapping the shoulders, slapping the knees,* or some other motion. All of the players immediately follow the leader as the motions change. The players casually watch the leader by glancing at him or her, so as not to give the leader away by staring. The center child's eyes are opened. He or she must discover who is leading the group's motions. As soon as the leader is discovered, a new center child and leader are selected.

Variation: *Electricity*   The children love the anticipation in this fast-moving game! The child who is *It* stands in the circle. While *Its* eyes are shut, point to someone to begin the electricity. All of the players hold hands. The leader squeezes the hand of one of the children next to him or her, who passes it on. The electricity can move to the left or right at any time. *It* observes carefully to locate the *Electrical Source.* When discovered, the Source of electricity *becomes* the new *It.*

Kitty capers

Develops: visual awareness
gross motor skills
listening skills
awareness of other players
imagination
laughter

Audience: toddler (E-1), preschool,
kindergarten, primary

Group Size: small group

Setting: circle time, playground (H),
dramatics, movement

Directions: A favorite pet for young children is a cat. Because children are so familiar with this soft, cuddly, friendly animal, it is easy and fun to imitate it.

Easier: 1. *Copy Cats*   The leader makes cat-like motions, such as: *stretching, walking on all fours, licking lips.* The players must copy. (Other animals or actions may also be imitated.)

2. *Poor Kitty*   The children sit in a circle. One child who is the *Kitty* crawls in front of a player and *meows* in a silly way to make him or her laugh. The player must look at the Kitty, pat it on the head, and say, *Poor Kitty.* They alternate *meow* and *Poor Kitty* three times. If the player laughs, he or she is the next Kitty. If not, the Kitty moves to another person. This is a wonderful game for concentration.

Harder: *Pussycat Wants a Corner*   Each of four players finds a corner of the room or playground. The fifth player is the *Pussycat* in the center. This youngster goes to a corner child, *meows*, and says, *Pussycat wants a corner.* The player replies, *Go next door.* After several refusals, Pussycat calls from the center, *Change places!* Players try to exchange corners while the Pussycat attempts to take one of their homes. Whoever is left without a corner becomes the next Pussycat.

Can you find?

Develops: visual discrimination
listening and following directions
understanding of cues
body awareness
positive self-image

Audience: toddler (E), preschool,
kindergarten

Group Size: individual, small or large group

Setting: lap, circle time, transition

Directions: To familiarize the children with body parts ask, for example: *Can you find your head, arm, or leg?* The children locate the feature and point to it in response to your verbal request. When the youngsters can easily identify simple, large features, name finer features—*nose, toes, fingers, mouth, ears.* Continue the game by requesting that the children point to various articles of clothing which cover their body parts. *Can you find your shoe?* If hints are necessary, add *It is on your foot.*

Easier: Make the request while holding the child in your lap or facing the child. Take his or her hand in yours and together touch the child's correct body part in order for the youngster to associate the word with the physical feature. This is an excellent cuddling game!

Harder: 1. Have the children close their eyes and point to the named body part. They may open their eyes to check if they touched the correct place.
2. Ask the children to locate a specific body part on someone else, for example, *Can you find Joe's shoulder?*

Variations: 1. Have a child find and touch very specific features on himself or herself (*a scratch, a green sweatshirt*) or on another classmate (*braids*).
2. Extend the game to objects in the classroom or playground, for example: *Can you find an easel?* Play this game outside—look for objects on the playground, for example, *Can you find the slide?*

Adaptations: After reading your lips, the hearing impaired child has an added advantage of observing where the other players are pointing as a visual check and may join the group in touching the appropriate place. The tactile stimulation is helpful for a blind child who may work with a partner.

Child sort

Develops: awareness of self and others
visual discrimination
listening skills
descriptive characterizing
concept of sets
comparative characterizing

Audience: preschool, kindergarten, primary

Group Size: large group

Setting: circle time, gym, seated at desks, math, social studies

Directions: Whenever the leader names a feature which describes them, the players must come to the center of the circle or the front of the room. The leader might call out *blue eyes* or *brown hair*, or something more specific: *wavy black hair, braids, freckles,* or *a square-shaped face.* After confirmation, the players return to their places. To keep the players alert, the leader periodically calls out *a nose, ten toes,* or *two elbows!* This game shows the players that while people may be different, they all have much in common. To extend the game, utilize various *types of clothing* worn by the players, as well as *clothing textures* or *special features: jackets with zippers* or *sneakers with velcro snaps.*

Harder: Discuss and describe sets, using examples of characteristics of children, for example, *those with brown eyes* or *those wearing glasses.* Call out several different groupings. Then, show the children how they might belong to more than one set (*brown eyes/blonde hair*). Have intersecting sets link arms.

Variation: Have a scorekeeper line up the number of children with specific features. For example, group the children into different sets according to *blue, black, brown,* and *hazel* eyes. Have them align themselves to create a human graph!

LOOK OUT!

Lost child

Develops: visual discrimination
descriptive characterizing
oral communication
self-awareness
listening skills
awareness of roles

Audience: preschool, kindergarten, primary

Group Size: large group

Setting: playground (V), gym (V), social studies, language, circle time

Directions: This game gives the children an opportunity to role-play a real-life situation in case they ever need to report information to a police officer. It also enables the children to consider the police officer a person who helps others. Have one child play the role of *Parent* and another, the *Police Officer*. Have the Parent and Police Officer stand in the center of a circle formed by the rest of the children. The Parent asks, *Officer, have you seen my child?* The Officer replies, *Tell me what your child looks like.* The parent describes the child, for example: *He has brown hair and is wearing a blue shirt.* The Officer points to a child in the circle who fits the description and asks, *Is this your child?* The Parent says, *Yes! Thank you for finding my lost child.* If this is not the lost child, the Parent continues to give clues as the Officer searches.

Variations: *Have You Seen My Sheep?* In this old-time game, one child is the *Shepherd* and asks a player in the circle, *Have you seen my sheep?* The player asks, *What does it look like?* The Shepherd describes another child, who is the *Lost Sheep.* When the player guesses who the Sheep is, the Shepherd says, *Yes, that is my Sheep!* The player chases the Sheep around the outside of the circle to bring it back to the Shepherd. The Sheep may run back to its safe place in the fold before the player catches it. The chaser becomes the new Shepherd.

Who is missing?

Develops: visual discrimination
group consciousness
awareness of positions
memory

Audience: toddler (small group), preschool, kindergarten, primary

Group Size: small or large group

Setting: circle time, at desks

Directions: The players sit in a circle. *It* sits in the center and covers his or her eyes. Point to a child to hide somewhere in the room. *It* opens his or her eyes and tries to guess who is missing. Depending upon the level of the players, allow *It* to have one, two, or three guesses. The missing child then changes places with *It*.

Harder: After the missing child has hidden, have all of the players quickly switch places before *It* guesses who is missing. (This is necessary if the players are sitting at assigned seats in desks.)

Variation: Change the game to *What Is Missing?* Have all the players close their eyes. *It* removes something, for example: *takes off a barrette* or *a sock; changes a necklace to the back.* The players then open their eyes and guess what is missing.

Adaptation: If *It* is visually impaired, he or she may ask, *Who is missing?* The missing child responds *I am. It* tries to guess who this child is from the voice. (Try this game variation with the entire class, too.)

Ready or not

Develops: visual discrimination
listening skills
sequencing skills
role reversal
awareness of other players

Audience: toddler (E), preschool (E),
kindergarten (E), primary

Group Size: pair (E), small or large group

Setting: outdoors, indoors (E, V)

Directions: This is a favorite outdoor game. Standing at a spot selected as home, *It* hides his or her eyes and counts slowly to a designated number (depending upon ability). The other players find hiding places. When *It* finishes counting, he or she yells, *Ready or not, here I come! It* cries out when he or she locates a hidden player, for example: *I spy Keisha.* They both run to touch home. If the player arrives first, he or she yells *Home free!* However, if *It* tags the player, *It* yells *Everyone home free!* All of the players come out of hiding and the tagged player becomes the new *It.*

Easier: *Hide and Seek*   This is a classic game played with an adult and child or a very small group. *It* covers his or her eyes while the others hide. When they call out *Ready, It* seeks their hiding places. If hints are needed, *It* might ask, *Are you hiding under the table?* The player responds *yes* or *no.*

Variation: *Sardines*   This game should be played where there are lots of roomy hiding places. A player is picked to be the *Sardine.* While the other players cover their eyes and count slowly to ten, the Sardine hides. Each player who finds the Sardine joins and hides with him or her until everyone is hiding together. The last Sardine becomes the next one to hide. Usually the Sardines end up laughing as they huddle together!

Colors

Develops: color discrimination
gross motor skills
awareness of other players
role reversal
listening skills

Audience: late preschool, kindergarten, primary

Group Size: small or large groups

Setting: playground, gym, circle time, language, movement

Directions: The youngsters sit in a circle. The leader names a color and a form of locomotion, for example: *red—skip* or *blue—hop*. The players wearing that color move around the outside of the circle, performing the particular action. The first child to return to his or her place becomes the next caller.

Variations: 1. *Color Tag* *It* calls out a color. Any child wearing that color *cannot* be tagged. (To keep the players alert, *It* may call out a color change. If tagged, a child becomes *It*.)
2. *If You Are Wearing Red* *It* remains a distance away from the other players who face the runner. A player yells to *It*, *May I chase you? It* replies, for example: *If you are wearing the color green*. These players run and try to tag *It*. If a player succeeds, he or she is the next *It*. For increased difficulty, *It* may call out a combination of two or more colors: *if you are wearing red and blue*.

Adaptation: For children who speak English as a second language, this is a good game to learn colors. The words may be called out and repeated in both languages.

I spy

Develops: visual discrimination
awareness of characteristics
verbal understanding
listening skills
concepts of size, shape, or color
beginning phonetics

Audience: preschool, kindergarten,
primary (H,V)

Group Size: pair, small or large group

Setting: circle time, transition, traveling,
language

Directions: The group decides ahead of time whether to use colors, items, shapes, or objects that begin with a specific letter. A player thinks of something that he or she can see. The other children attempt to guess what it is by asking questions that can be answered by *yes* or *no*. For example, if the player says: *I spy with my little eye something red*, the players might guess, *Diane's sweater*. The guesser thinks of the next *I spy* object. This is one of the best traveling or waiting games.

Easier: Limit the players' choices to objects in a specified area: *the toy shelf, the children in the circle, the teacher's desk, or the inside of the car.*

Harder: The player relates, for example: *I spy with my little eye something that rhymes with cat (hat).*

Variation: *Make-believe I Spy*   The person who is *It* pretends to hide somewhere in the area that can be seen by the children. For example, in his or her imagination, *It may be hiding on the chalk tray* or *in the paint jar*. Hints are given if necessary. The players guess and *It* answers *yes* or *no*, until someone guesses the hiding place.

I saw

Develops: visual memory
alertness to cues
concepts of place and position
language

Audience: toddler (E), preschool,
kindergarten, primary (H,V)

Group Size: pair, small or large group

Setting: circle time, traveling, language

Directions: Invite the children to face a particular area, e.g. a side of the room, the front of a car, or a box of toys. Ask the players to look carefully at everything. Have them close their eyes. Ask, *What did you see?* Give each player a chance to respond, for example: *I saw a clock. I saw a radio.* A scorekeeper counts how many items are mentioned.

Easier: Each player focuses on another child or one specific object, then shuts his or her eyes. Ask, *What did you see?* The youngster responds, *I saw a pony tail, I saw blue eyes,* and continues mentioning as many characteristics as possible. When the player needs assistance, ask him or her a question, *Was (Roger) wearing a sweater?* (If the children are not sure, allow them to peek to confirm the answer.)

Harder: *What's Missing?*   After the players have listed observed items, remove one object. Ask them to open their eyes, look around and tell what is missing.

Variation: *Alterations*   Select a team of movers. The rest of the players observe the area for a designated period; then, shut their eyes. The team of movers changes several objects around, for example: flip the calendar to a new page or move a plant to the other side of the windowsill. You might tell the players how many things were changed. The players try to guess the alterations after they open their eyes.

Adaptation: Give the visually impaired child a chance to touch various objects in the selected area. He or she then describes them to the other players.

Action! Camera!

Develops: visual discrimination
descriptive characterizing
oral communication
listening skills
imagination (V)
thinking skills

Audience: preschool, kindergarten, primary

Group Size: pair, small or large group

Setting: transition, circle time, language
dramatics (V), traveling

Directions: This is a favorite game whenever children must sit and wait for a short time. The child designated as the *Photographer* takes a picture of an object in the room with a *Magic Camera* by giving descriptive clues. The players try to guess the item. If they cannot, the Photographer continues to shoot his or her roll of film by giving pictorial hints until the item is named. The child who guesses correctly becomes the next Photographer—a popular role!

Easier: The Photographer secretly takes a picture of a child in the group. He or she then gives clues to the others to the child's identity. The players try to guess who is the *Subject* from the Photographer's descriptive hints.

Harder: The *Camera Technician* describes a scene while shooting footage for a movie. The audience must guess where the action is taking place.

Variation: Have the players discuss how they will act out the plot for their new TV program. Then rehearse it in front of imaginary TV cameras.

Hey, look me over!

Develops: visual discrimination
oral communication
role reversal
social interaction
memory
descriptive characterizing

Audience: late preschool (E), kindergarten, primary (H)

Group Size: pairs

Setting: circle time, transition, language

Directions: Have the children select partners. Then give them ample time to carefully look each other over. Next, have the partners turn so that they are back-to-back. One partner asks the other questions, for example: *Do I have blue eyes?* or *Am I wearing a sweater?* The respondent answers *yes* or *no*. If the respondent is not sure, the player may turn around to check. The child who asks the questions may state any nonsensical characteristic: *Do I have green hair? Do I have pink and purple spots?* Be sure to have the children switch roles. This is a terrific game to help children get to know each other. They are certain to giggle when their partners ask silly questions!

Easier: Have the children limit the questions to a specific category, such as *clothing* or *physical features.*

Harder: After an observation period, the partners turn back-to-back and switch an item that they are wearing. Some suggestions may include: *changing a watch to the other wrist, rolling down a sock,* or *taking off eyeglasses.* They then turn towards each other and try to guess the missing or changed item. Each time the children play this game, they sharpen skills in visual discrimination.

Adaptation: This is a favorite ice-breaker for parent meetings. The parents quickly see how important their children's observation skills are.

What am I saying?

Develops: visual discrimination
concentration
decoding
dramatization (V)
awareness of others' actions
language

Audience: late preschool (E), kindergarten, primary

Group Size: pairs or small group

Setting: language, circle time, dramatics (V), traveling

Directions: Have pairs of players sit closely together facing each other. Tell the children how important it is to say words carefully so that people understand. Explain that some people do not hear well and must rely on lip reading. Have the pairs of players practice mouthing various common words to see if each can guess what the other is saying by reading the person's lips. Start off by using categories to make the guessing easier. This is a very quiet and intense activity.

Easier: Read a sentence out loud, saying all the words in it except for one. The players must lip read and figure out the missing word from the context of the sentence.

Variation: Have one pair dramatize an object or action word. The other pairs guess what the pair is saying.

Adaptation: Invite a resource person to explain to the youngsters how people who cannot hear find out what others are saying by lip reading or using sign language. Give the children a chance to learn and practice some special words by signing them. *I love you* is an easy phrase to sign.

Pick a property

Develops: visual discrimination
classification skills
verbal comprehension
language

Audience: preschool, kindergarten, primary

Group Size: pair, small or large group

Setting: circle time, seated at desks,
while waiting

Directions: You or a child give a specific property, such as: *wood, glass, paper, metal* or *plastic*. The other children look around the room and try to guess the specific object containing the named property.

Easier: Continue to use only one property until the youngsters recognize it easily.

Harder: Guess an object containing property combinations. For example, a *window* contains both *glass* and *wood*.

Variations: 1. Name an object. Have the students tell its various properties.
2. If the children need physical activity, have them get up and touch various objects with the specific property that has been chosen.

Adaptations: If English is a second language for the children, show them several examples of objects containing a desired property. Have them walk around the room and touch other objects with this property. As the objects are touched, you may say the names to familiarize the children with new words.

Shape add-ons

Develops: shape recognition
visual discrimination
memory
following directions
alertness to sensory cues
sequencing skills

Audience: preschool (E), kindergarten, primary

Group Size: pair, small or large group

Setting: circle time, seated at desks, outdoors, math

Directions: Name a specific *geometric shape.* The first child locates something with that shape, for example: *rectangle—door* or *picture frame.* The child touches the object and then returns to his or her place. The next player touches the same object and adds another item with that same shape. The following child touches a third object with the shape, and so on, until the players can no longer find an item, or are unable to remember the sequence. If practice is needed, begin again with the same shape. Try other shapes.

Easier: Name a shape and point to several examples. Have the children take turns naming or touching objects with that same shape.

Harder: 1. Include some less common shapes, like an *octagon* (*a stop sign*) or a *pentagon* (*a birdhouse*).
2. Have the group determine add-on shape patterns—*circle, square, circle, square (clock, window, jar lid, book).*

Variation: A variety of categories can be used, such as: *colors, textures, toys, things that make noise, objects that roll,* and *items that begin or end with a specific sound.*

Adaptations: Allow the physically challenged child to work with another child who is able to move around the room easily. If English is a second language for a youngster, name the objects as they are touched to stimulate language development. The visually impaired youngster can be paired with a sighted child. The sighted child acts as a guide throughout the sequence as the visually impaired child discovers shapes through touch.

Larger than your thumb

Develops: body awareness
visual discrimination
size concepts
large/small space judgment
comparison skills
problem-solving

Audience: preschool (E), kindergarten (E), primary

Group Size: individual, pair, small or large group

Setting: a defined area: a classroom, cafeteria, school bus; or circle time, math, while waiting

Directions: Have one child think of something in the room that is *larger than his or her thumb, but smaller than his or her hand*. This child gives clues, while the rest of the children try to guess this object.

Easier: After the youngsters have been given directions, allow them to confirm their findings. Have players take turns walking around the room and placing their thumbs and hands next to various objects for a comparison.

Harder: Ask the children to estimate how many objects they will find. Work as a group to verbally list all of the objects they can see that are larger than their thumbs yet smaller than their hands. Were they close to their estimates?

Variations: A variety of comparisons can be used. Some suggestions may include: *larger than your nose, but smaller than your face; longer than your hand, but shorter than your arm; taller than a specific child, but shorter than the leader.*

Adaptations: The visually impaired child may feel the objects that he or she is comparing. A confident child can be paired with a child who has low self-esteem.

It's handy

Develops: visual discrimination
thinking skills
descriptive characterizing
body awareness
visual-motor skills (V)
imagination

Directions: See how many things the players can think of to do with their hands (*wave, eat, brush their teeth, draw pictures*). For a challenge, ask one child to pantomime a hand action, perhaps rowing a boat, while the others try to guess what the hands are doing.

Harder: Have a hand contest. Guess who has the: *longest hands, shortest hands, widest hands, biggest hands, or hands wearing the most rings.* After speculating, allow the players to compare hands to verify their predictions. They may be surprised!

Audience: preschool, kindergarten, primary (H,V)

Group Size: individual (V), small or large group

Setting: circle time, self-awareness, language, dramatics, transition (V), traveling (V)

Variation: *Whoops, Johnny* is a nonsensical hand game. Each child holds up one palm and spreads the fingers apart. With the opposite index finger, he or she begins by touching the pinky and saying, *Johnny*, and continues with each finger, through the index finger. After touching the index finger, the pointer finger slides down, then up the thumb, as the child says *Whoops!* The top of the thumb is tapped as the player repeats, *Johnny.* The entire process, starting with the thumb, is reversed. Players try to see how fast they can play this silly hand game before they become mixed up.

LISTEN AND SAY

Auditory and oral communication games help the youngsters to strengthen their listening skills and express themselves meaningfully as they interact during verbal activities. Through game playing, the children develop auditory discrimination by identifying, matching, or reproducing sounds and patterns. The players quickly learn to listen for verbal clues and follow spoken directions. While becoming familiar with the process of giving and receiving important information during the games, the children expand their vocabularies. Certain activities in this chapter encourage them to practice the delightful art of storytelling and interpreting characters' roles.

Nursery rhyme time

Develops: language
listening skills
familiarity with nursery rhymes
creative thinking (H)
imagination (V)
memory
decoding skills

Audience: preschool, kindergarten,
primary (H)

Group Size: pair, small or large group

Setting: language, circle time, transition,
traveling, dramatics (V)

Directions: Repeat the first line or two of a
nursery rhyme. The children try to fill in the
rest of the lines of the rhyme and say the
name of the rhyme.

Easier: Recite an entire nursery rhyme,
substituting a child's name in the verse. The
players try to guess the title of the rhyme.
For example, the following uses the rhyme
Mary, Mary Quite Contrary:

> Lois, Lois Piermattei
> How does your garden grow?
> With silver bells and cockle shells
> And pretty maids all in a row.

Harder: After reciting several lines of a
nursery rhyme, ask the children to make up
their own line, for example:

> Little Jack Horner sat in the corner,
> Eating his Christmas pie.
> He put in his thumb and
> Pulled out a plum,
> And said I'm a good boy, my oh my!

Variation: Whisper a nursery rhyme to a
small group. Let them act out the rhyme for
the rest of the class, who must guess the
nursery rhyme.

Rhyme time

Develops: language
            auditory discrimination
            thinking skills
            turn taking

Audience: toddler (E), preschool,
            kindergarten (H,V)

Group Size: pair, small group

Setting: language, circle time, transition

Directions: The person who is *It* sits in the center of the circle and says a simple word, for example: *at.* It points to a player who must offer a word that rhymes with *at*, for example: *cat.* If the player gives an appropriate response, It points to another player for a rhyming word. If a player does not answer with a rhyme, he or she becomes the new It. Offer assistance if the players have difficulty thinking of simple rhyming words.

Easier: Play with one player. The child suggests a word or a nonsense phrase like *fu-fu!* You respond with a silly rhyming word, *su-su.* The players banter back and forth repeating these silly rhymes. At a suitable point, add another rhyming word, *tu-tu.* This is a funny, face-to-face game!

Harder: The person who is It says, for example: *I am thinking of a word that rhymes with see.* A player asks for simple hints, for example: *Does it sting?* It replies, *No, it is not a bee.* Another player asks, *Does it have leaves?* It agrees, *Yes, it is a tree.*

Variation: The leader recites a line to the other players. They offer different rhyming lines.

     Leader: *Knock, knock on the door.*
     Player 1: *Come in and sit on the floor.*
     Leader: *Knock, knock on the door.*
     Player 2: *Let me in, the lion said with a roar.*

Ring-a-ling

Develops: oral communication
listening skills
imagination
thinking skills
role reversal
ritualized sequencing
practice to extend growth

Audience: toddler, preschool (H),
kindergarten (H), primary (V)

Group Size: pair

Setting: language, dramatics, self-awareness

Directions: *Telephone Ritual* Young children adore talking on the telephone with all of the ritual involved. It makes them feel very grown-up to imitate an adult telephoning. Both players use pretend phones. The first player dials and says *Ring-a-ling*. The other child says *Hello*. The caller replies, *Hello*. The youngsters carry on a conversation appropriate for their level. It may be as simple as *How are you?* or *I love you!* Their talk ends with *Good-bye.*

Harder: Suggest a theme for the telephone talk, such as: *going to the store, getting ready for a trip, making bread,* or *describing a favorite toy* or *game.* Help the children in advance to think of related questions if they need assistance.

Variation: *Telephone Emergency* This game gives the players an opportunity to practice giving and receiving important information. The children learn to dial 0 (or 911). One child plays the *Operator.* When he or she asks questions, another child answers, stating clearly *name, parent's names, address,* or *phone number.*

Fill in the sound

Develops: listening skills
memory
oral communication
imagination
understanding of cues
awareness of roles

Audience: toddler (E), preschool,
kindergarten, primary (V)

Group Size: small or large group

Setting: circle time, language,
dramatics

Directions: Select volunteers to be different sounds before telling a story. Explain that when the *Storyteller* gets to a certain part in the story, the child assigned to that role makes the appropriate sound. Several players may choose the same sound if the group is large. An example of a sound story using farm animals might begin: Once upon a time, the farmer and his wife needed an alarm clock, so they bought a rooster (children assigned to make rooster sounds, chime in), *cock-a-doodle-doo*. The rooster, *cock-a-doodle-doo*, also woke up the sleepy pigs, *oink-oink*, in their pen, and so on.

Easier: Allow the players to hear and practice their sounds before telling the story. If children need hints, point to them when it is their turn to make sounds.

Harder: Make the sound story a group effort. As each character is named in the story, have all of the players respond with the specific sound.

Variation: 1. Tell stories that invite silly sounds, such as: machines (an egg beater—*whir, whir*), unrelated sounds (lion—*roar*, a rocking chair—*squeak, squeak*) and nonsense characters (a pooka—*rattle, hiss*). 2. During Halloween, or around a campfire, narrate stories using scary sounds, i.e.: *creaking doors, a booing ghost*, and so on. 3. The character dramatizes the sound as he or she verbalizes it.

A cooperative story

Develops: language development
listening skills
divergent thinking
sense of humor
awareness of others' ideas

Audience: preschool (E), kindergarten, primary

Group Size: pair (adult and child), small or large group

Setting: circle time, desks, language time, traveling

Directions: The leader begins a story any way that he or she chooses. It develops as a cooperative group effort; therefore, it is different every time! To indicate that the story is make-believe, the leader starts with, *Once upon a time....* A player then adds a phrase. The leader continues with a sentence, then has each player fill in additional remarks. The players' turns may be taken clockwise in the circle or the leader may decide to point to different children randomly in order to keep them alert. For example:

> Leader: Once upon a time there was a . . .
> Player: great big bear . . .
> Leader: who lived in . . .
> Player: a cave in the forest . . .

Children love silly stories. This same story might be told this way:

> Leader: Once upon a time there was a . . .
> Player: big, green, polka-dotted pooka . . .
> Leader: who lived in . . .
> Player: a bowl of jiggly, red gelatin . . .

Easier: The leader tells the major portion of the story. The youngsters fill in only one word.

Harder: The players must supply one or more story sentences until stopped by the leader, who then points to the next storyteller to continue.

Variation: Instead of verbally filling in a word, phrase, or sentence, the players pantomime their responses.

Yes, no or maybe

Develops: oral communication
thinking skills
simple choice-making
listening skills

Audience: toddler (E), preschool,
kindergarten, primary

Group Size: pair, small or large group

Setting: circle time, transition, traveling,
language

Directions: The leader asks an individual child, or the entire group, questions which must be answered with *yes, no*, or *maybe*. Sample questions may include: *Is it raining?*, *Did you eat peas for lunch?*, or *Will your father pick you up after school today?* For quick turnover, if the respondent answers correctly, he or she becomes the new leader.

Easier: Use questions about things that the players can easily *observe, hear, taste, touch,* or *smell*. Here are some suggestions: *Are you wearing shoes with buckles?*, *Can you hear the clock tick?*, or *Is the rug rough?*

Harder: The leader inquires about concepts familiar to the children, for example: *Do carrots grow in the ground?*, *Are cats, dogs and tulips all animals?* or *Does a jacket have buttons?*

Variations: 1. The players reply to various questions as if they are someone or something else. Either you select the person or thing or have the children select someone. For example, the children might answer all questions as *Winnie-the-Pooh— Do you like honey? Yes! Do you like to ride bicycles? No! Do you like bees? No!*
2. The leader selects a *response* (NO). He or she points to a child who has to think up an appropriate question: *Does a refrigerator keep food hot?*

Another way to say

Develops: oral communication
alertness to sensory cues
ability to characterize
thinking skills
social interaction
imagination

Audience: toddler, preschool, kindergarten, primary

Group Size: individual, small or large group

Setting: snack, transition, circle time, seated at desks, language, traveling

Directions: This game is especially fun to play during snacks or meals. It is a favorite of many children. After they have had the opportunity to make, handle, observe and eat a food, such as a cookie, the teacher says, *Can you tell how this tastes?* They usually respond, *Good!* Then ask them to describe the food another way. Responses may include: *yummy, delicious, wonderful and squishy!* For several days in a row, encourage the players to expand their vocabularies by playing *Another Way* with new foods. Are the descriptions similar? Different? Ask the players to use a variety of words to describe other items (*toys or clothes*).

Harder: 1. Play *Another Way* by saying abstract words, for example: *said— explained, whispered, and replied.*
2. Utilize descriptive phrases to explain an item in another way, for example, *a ball: a round bouncy circle.*

Adaptation: In order to enhance each child's self-image, focus on a specific child. Suggest a positive description for this child: *helpful.* Ask the players for others: *pretty, kind, artistic,* and so on.

Attributes

Develops: oral communication
ability to characterize
listening skills
thinking skills

Audience: preschool (E), kindergarten, primary

Group Size: individual, pair, small or large group

Setting: snack or meal time, circle time, transition, seated at desks

Directions: Discuss with children that an *Attribute* is something special that helps to describe a particular object. Then, select an object that the children are familiar with or have had an opportunity to handle (*an apple at snack time*). For example, *the attributes of an apple include the following: round, juicy, crunchy, red, white inside, has seeds*. The children take turns going around the circle naming additional attributes. (Decide ahead of time whether hints may be given, such as, *Does an apple roll?*)

Easier: Play this game during snack time so that the children have a hands-on, sensory experience with a specific food item, while they discuss it.

Harder: Select any category such as: fruit, transportation, shelter. Have the youngsters describe various attributes of particular items in the category. For example, using the category *transportation*, the children name objects and attributes: *boat—floats, has a bottom, has an engine; airplane—flies, carries people, has an engine*. At the end of the game, have the players discuss the attributes that the items have in common.

Variation: One child thinks of an object and names an attribute. The group tries to guess the object. The child continues listing attributes until the others guess the item. (You might need to provide clues.)

Adaptation: Whenever possible, give the visually impaired player an opportunity to handle the item first or during the game.

Whisper

Develops: listening skills
auditory decoding
oral communication
social interaction
a sense of humor

Audience: toddler (E), preschool
(small group), kindergarten,
primary

Group Size: pair (E), small or large group

Setting: a great ice breaker, circle time,
language, dramatics (V)

Directions: Have the players sit in a circle or stand in a line. Have one child clearly whisper a word or phrase to the person sitting or standing next to him or her. This comment is whispered along. The last person repeats the phrase out loud to the group to see if it matches the original statement. Sometimes the results are very strange and funny! (To develop good listening skills, emphasize that the comment will be whispered only once to each person).

Easier: Play in pairs. One player whispers a simple word to the other. The recipient says it as soon as he or she hears it. This can also be a wonderful, giggly lap game between you and the child.

Variation: Whisper a phrase that can be acted out. The first player in the circle passes it along to the next player. (A message might be: *to hop on one foot and pat your head*). The last recipient dramatizes the message. The group verifies whether or not this is the original statement!

Harder: 1. Whisper a complete sentence. See if it gets passed correctly all the way down the line.
2. Think of a nonsense phrase to whisper, for example: *hocus-pocus-holy-smokus* and send it around the circle.

Don't say it!

Develops: oral communication
social interaction
listening skills
thinking skills
number concepts (V)
impulse control

Audience: kindergarten, primary, older primary (V)

Group Size: small or large group

Setting: circle time, language, math, traveling

Directions: The players agree not to say a specific word—a simple word used frequently in conversation, such as *yes, no* or *I.* The children try to trick each other into saying the word by engaging in conversation or asking each other questions. For example, if the word selected is *yes*, a person might ask another player, *Do you like peanut butter sandwiches?* When one player outfoxes another, laughter usually follows!

Variation: *Buzz*   This is an old math favorite. The children sit in a circle. The first child begins counting. Each player continues counting around the group. When the number seven occurs, any number containing seven (17, 71), or any multiple of seven (4 × 7 = 28), the players don't say it. Instead, the youngster whose turn it is must substitute the word *buzz*. If the player forgets to say *buzz* for a seven number, he or she moves to the center of the circle. This player then exchanges places with the next child who doesn't say *buzz* at the appropriate time.

Alarm clock

Develops: listening skills
directionality

Audience: toddler (E), preschool,
kindergarten, primary

Group Size: pair, small or large group

Setting: circle time, can be adapted for
play at desks

Directions: The child designated as *It* sits in the center of the circle with his or her eyes shut. A player representing the *Clock* stands anywhere he or she chooses in the room. In a loud voice, the Clock says *tick-tock-tick-tock*. After listening carefully, *It* tries to point to the spot where the Clock is standing. If *It* is correct, the Clock rings an alarm, *brrring* and *It* becomes the new clock. (Sometimes, *It* needs another chance to listen for the clock's sound.)

Easier: The child who is *It* closes his or her eyes and sits in the center of a circle of children. You choose one child to play the Clock by tapping him or her on the head. Without leaving the circle, this player makes the Clock's sound. (If the players are very young, the Clock should tick steadily). The child who is *It* tries to guess who is the clock.

Harder: You turn *It* (with eyes shut) around several times. Another child, designated as the Clock, says *tick-tock*. *It* then points in the direction of the sound.

Variation: Use themes for the sound: farm animals—*mooo-mooo* (cow), *meow* (cat); machinery—*buzzzz* (chain saw), or *bang* (hammer).

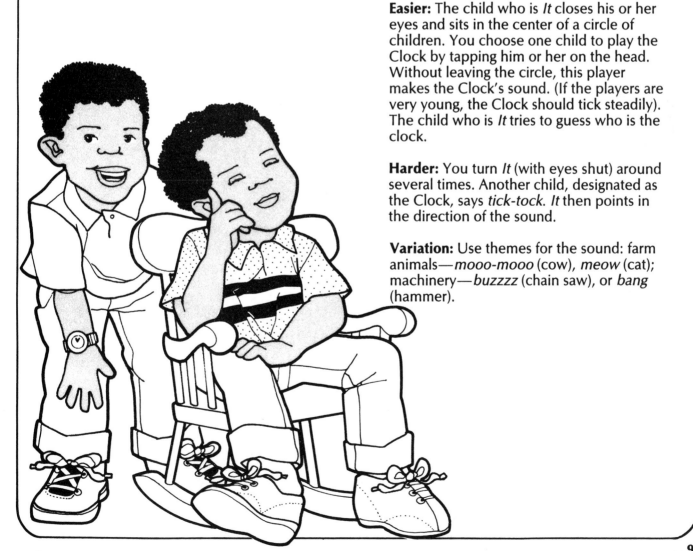

Knock! Knock!

Develops: listening skills
awareness of direction
discrimination
thinking skills

Audience: toddler (E), preschool (E),
kindergarten, primary

Group Size: pair, small or large group

Setting: classroom, circle time, science

Directions: All of the players close their eyes while *It* knocks three times on a particular object in the room. *It* then walks quietly to the center and says, *Knock, knock.* The players open their eyes and try to guess the object that was knocked. The person who guesses correctly becomes the next It.

Easier: Select several objects in the class, for example: a wooden table or metal chair. Allow the children to practice knocking on them to hear the different sounds that they make. Ask them to close their eyes. Knock on one of the items. The children tell which item it is. Ask them to close their eyes. They may then open their eyes to check their guesses.

Variation: The children close their eyes. *It* makes sounds in various ways, such as *clapping hands, slapping thighs, stamping feet, scratching a tissue box with a fingernail, or tapping a book with a finger.* With eyes still closed, the players must identify the sound. Afterwards, they may enjoy repeating the sounds.

Adaptation: For the child who speaks English as a second language, touch the item guessed. You give the response in English. The player names it in his or her language.

I hear

Develops: listening skills
         describing characteristics
         thinking skills

Audience: toddler (E), preschool, kindergarten, primary (V,H)

Group Size: pair, small or large group

Setting: outdoors, circle time, transition, language

Directions: This game is played in a similar fashion to the old favorite *I Spy With My Little Eye*. The challenger says, *I hear something with my little ear* and gives hints, such as, *It is loud* or *It is low.* The players try to make the sound and guess the object.

Easier: Name only objects that can be seen by the players. Broad clues should be given, such as: *It says tick-tock* (for a clock), or *a thing you beat* (for a drum).

Harder: Vary the game. Some suggestions are: *I hear with my little ear: a word with a short e vowel sound in the middle (pet),* or *a word that has two syllables (chicken).*

Variations: Utilize words from the children's spelling or reading vocabulary lists. The challenger states, for example, *I hear with my little ear: a word that begins with the same sound as ch.* The other players try to guess the word using their spelling list *(church).* The challenger might state other words: *ends with the same sound as d (band)* or *rhymes with the same sound as cat (bat).*

Adaptation: To enhance a child's self-image and personalize the game variation, the challenger may say, *I hear with my little ear a word that begins with the same sound as Lucille's name (love).*

Clap a pattern

Develops: auditory discrimination
sequencing skills
reproduction of sound patterns
hand coordination
body awareness

Audience: toddler (E), preschool (E),
kindergarten, primary (H)

Group Size: pair, small or large group

Setting: pair (sitting opposite each other),
circle time, seated at desks

Directions: In order to reproduce a pattern, the children repeat a variety of different claps, for example: *loud/soft, quick succession/spaced apart.*

Easier: Begin simply with a two-clap pattern. Have the youngsters duplicate it. Vary it with a soft-then-loud clap or lengthen the pause between the claps. Try adding another clap. Vary the three-clap pattern. Allow each child a chance to be the leader.

Harder: 1. Have the leader continue adding various claps to the pattern until the group is no longer able to repeat it. Then, start all over again!
2. Let each child in the circle take a turn repeating the varied pattern. He or she adds another clap and then the child on the right tries to duplicate it. See how long it can be repeated—then try it again!

Variation: Add a *foot stamp, knee slap, finger snap,* or any creative body movement to the pattern.

Adaptation: For physically challenged or hearing impaired children (or as another variation), *sing* different *la-la-la* patterns instead of clapping.

Name clap

Develops: listening skills/discrimination
classification
memory
patterning
positive self-image
rhythm
action-word coordination

Audience: older preschoolers,
kindergarten, primary

Group Size: small (6) or large group

Setting: circle time, language arts,
seated at desks, music (V)

Directions: Say a child's name. The children can tell how many beats are in the name. Have the children clap the beat(s) in the child's name along with you. Do this with each youngster's name. Have a child stand up. Clap his name, for example: *Juan.* Then invite all of the children whose names have the same number of beats as Juan to stand up. Have them clap their names for confirmation. Continue this with names of various beats, for example: *Wilfred—two; Gregory—three* and *Mary Ellen—four.*

Harder: Explain to the students that the beats in each word are called *syllables.* Use their spelling word list for the week or new reading vocabulary words. Have one child clap the syllables in a word. Ask the others to guess which word is represented by the claps.

Variation: Line up four to six youngsters. Explain that the audience will create a song by clapping the pattern of beats in this group's names, for example: *Julio—3, Ruby—2, Ramona—3, Luis—2.* The band leader may vary the tune by: speeding up the claps during the third and fourth time around or clapping the pattern of beats loudly the first and third times, softly the second and fourth time around. For a new song, rearrange the children or select four to six new children.

Hum along

Develops: auditory discrimination
familiarity with simple melodies
decoding skills
memory

Audience: toddler (E), preschool,
kindergarten, primary

Group Size: pair, small or large group

Setting: music, circle time, seated at desks,
transition, traveling, or language

Directions: The leader hums a song that is familiar to the children. They raise their hands when they recognize the tune, then tell the singer the song title.

Easier: For pure enjoyment with a young child, have him or her create a little humming sound. Quickly mimic the song. If the child creates it again, repeat it. The youngster will be delighted that you can hum his or her song, and will probably continue to make original sounds for you to copy!

Harder: Encourage the children to be song leaders. As soon as a tune is guessed, that child becomes the next hummer.

Variation: The first person in a line of children quietly hums a line of a song to the next person, who quickly passes it along. The last person hums the tune out loud to the first person to find out if the tune was passed along the line correctly.

Match the tone

Develops: auditory discrimination
awareness of self and others
memory
language
singing skills

Audience: toddler, preschool, kindergarten, primary (H)

Group Size: pair, small or large group

Setting: circle time, music, transition

Directions: Sing each child's name using different tones. The children duplicate the song by matching the tones. If necessary, repeat for accuracy. For a challenge, use first and last names.

Harder: 1. Use one child's name several times in a row. Alternate high and low tones to create a pattern for the children to match.
2. Develop a group song by utilizing a rapid *call and response* technique. First, quickly sing one child's name. The players match the tone. Then sing the next child's name. Continue several times around the group until the children are actually singing a name song.

Variation: Identify animals. Then sing various animal sounds using different tones, for example: *pig—oink, oink; lamb—baaa, baaa; rooster—cock-a-doodle-doo.* The players match the tones.

Adaptation: Hold a child who needs individual attention on your lap. Sing his or her name in a variety of ways. This makes the child feel very special!

Loud and quiet

Develops: auditory discrimination
ability to comprehend instructions
thinking skills
transforming situations
classifying

Audience: toddler (E), preschool,
kindergarten, primary

Group Size: pair, small or large group

Setting: circle time, transition, gym,
language

Directions: A child names items which make loud or quiet sounds. As a group, the others create the sound suggested by each item. Loud noises could include some of the following: *a chain saw*, *an elephant trumpeting*, *a motorcycle*, and *a drummer*. Quiet sounds might be: *a gentle breeze*, *a bunch of baby chicks*, *a fish blowing bubbles*, and *a kitten purring*. This game is a wonderful energy releaser! It allows the youngsters to yell loudly. The leader may also quiet the group instantly by shifting to a soft sound.

Easier: Create the sounds first, then have the children imitate them.

Variation: The players dramatize the sounds as they yell the loud ones or whisper the quiet ones. This is a great rainy day game when the children need to move around.

Do what I say

Develops: listening skills
action-word coordination
visual discrimination
fine motor skills
body awareness

Audience: toddler (E), preschool (E),
late kindergarten, primary

Group Size: pair, small or large group

Setting: circle time, language,
self-awareness

Directions: The players sit or stand across from the leader. The object of the game is for the players to *point to the body feature that you say*, rather than the body part that you are touching. For example: Point to your nose and repeat, *nose, nose, nose*. Quickly change to touch a different body part, such as the ear, but continue to call out *nose, nose, nose*. (The players point to this feature.) You might then switch and say, *hair, hair, hair*, but point to the elbow. (The players point to the hair.) If a player points to the wrong named feature, he or she becomes the new leader.

Easier: Point to a body part and name it *three times*. The players watch and listen carefully, then repeat the name three times. Continue to point and name other body parts. The children repeat the names.

Variation: Reverse the focus of the game. The players instead point to where the leader is touching and repeat the name three times.

Go!

Develops: listening skills
action-word coordination
comprehension of instructions
gross motor skills

Audience: toddler (E), preschool,
kindergarten, primary

Group Size: pair, small or large group

Setting: transition, movement, circle time,
playground (V), gym (V)

Directions: Announce two-step directions for the players to follow, for example: *Go to the wall and touch it.* (The phrase may be made specific, such as: *Go to the wall and touch it with your elbow.*) Directions may also be individualized: *Emma, go to the chair and sit down.* This game works well in getting the children ready to move to their next activity, for example, *Everyone who is wearing red, go line up at the door for outdoor play.*

Easier: Use one-step directions, *Go to the tree.*

Harder: Give three-step directions: *Malcolm, go to the table, pick up the book, and bring it to Michelle.*

Variations: Utilize specific means of locomotion in the directions. Ask the children to go by means of: *running, skipping, jumping, hopping on one foot, crawling on both knees, or taking baby steps.*
Go and Stop Here is a wonderful listening and movement game that works well in a large space. Issue the children commands to *go* then *stop* then *go* then *stop.* The children move on go and halt on stop. Space apart the *stop* and *go.* (Caution the children not to bump into each other.) Suggest they move by any predetermined method of locomotion, such as: *skipping, hopping, walking backwards,* and so on. This is a great energy releaser!

Find your partner

Develops: listening skills
directionality
gross motor skills
decoding skills
awareness of self in space
awareness of others' actions

Audience: preschool, kindergarten, primary (H)

Group Size: small or large group

Setting: gym, playground, movement

Directions: Each child chooses a partner. When you say *Go,* the players move far away from their partner by *running, skipping* or *twirling.* Suddenly, announce, *Freeze!* Everyone stops. Then continue with, *Find your partner!* The players scurry to locate him or her and hold hands. The youngsters enjoy moving quickly in this game.

Harder: *The Barnyard*   Divide the children into several groups of equal number. Each group selects a particular barnyard animal. One animal from each group goes out into the barnyard (different corners of the room). All of the other players remain in the center with their eyes shut. The animals in the barnyard begin to make animal noises. With eyes still shut and arms out in front of them, so as not to bump anyone, all of the animals must locate the animal from their group by following the appropriate barnyard noise. When they arrive at the correct barnyard, they make animal sounds, as well. When all the animals have found their group members, the game begins again and new animals go to the barnyard.

Fish swim

Develops: listening skills
mental alertness
classification skills
action-word coordination
awareness of others' actions
sense of humor

Audience: preschool, kindergarten, primary

Group Size: pair, small or large group

Setting: classroom, gym, playground, circle time, movement, transition, science

Directions: Begin by saying, *Fish swim!* Then make a swimming motion. The group repeats this phrase and imitates the swimming motion. Continue to name other animals that swim, i.e.: *a duck, a frog, a turtle*, followed by the swimming action. Periodically, name a non-swimming animal, *a bunny, a cat*, while adding the swimming motion. As soon as the children realize that this animal does not swim, they shout, *No!* and describe the animal's preferred locomotion, *bunny—hop*. To extend this game, have the players dramatize the correct motion.

Easier: Follow the above directions but make the distractor obvious; use very silly objects, such as *a chair* or *a book*. This always produces lots of giggles!

Variations: Instead of *Fish swim!*, use other animal categories, such as *birds (butterflies, ducks) fly*: children flap wings; *turtles (snakes, snails) crawl*: children make plodding motions with hands. The leader may dramatize the motions of other things: *tops (records, merry-go-rounds) spin*: children turn round and round; or, *flowers (boys, carrots) grow*: children reach hands over head for "so big" motion.

Adaptation: This game offers the physically challenged child a chance to exercise and strengthen his or her arm muscles with the other children. Position the hearing impaired child so he or she can easily read the leader's lips, and is not tricked when the motion does not relate to the animal or object.

Duck, duck, goose

Develops: listening skills
awareness of others' actions
practice of spelling words (H)
alertness to sensory clues
gross motor skills
language

Audience: preschool, kindergarten,
primary (H,V)

Group Size: one or two small groups

Setting: language, playground, gym,
circle time, movement

Directions: This modified version of the old favorite is designed so that everyone quickly has a turn to be the *Goose*. The players sit or kneel in a circle. The Goose walks around the circle, gently tapping the players on the head while repeating *duck*. After a few taps, the Goose finally says, *goose*. The tapped player runs around the circle after the Goose. If the Goose arrives at the empty place first, the chaser becomes the new Goose. If the Goose is tagged, he or she sits in the *duck pond*, the center, for a turn. The chaser becomes the Goose. (A word of caution when playing this often requested game. The group must be small so that everyone receives a turn quickly. If the group is large, divide it into two small groups and play separate games.)

Harder: *Spelling Goose*   The Goose announces a spelling word, for example, *bed*; and spells the word as he or she taps the players (*b-e-d*). On the last letter of the spelling word, the tapped player chases the Goose around the circle.

Variation: *Shake Hands*   The players put their hands behind their backs as the Goose walks around the circle and taps a selected player's hands. This player and the Goose race in opposite directions. When they meet, they shake hands, then continue racing to see who reaches the vacant spot first and sits down. The one left standing becomes the next Goose.

Mother/Father has a headache

Develops: listening skills
directionality
sequence of movement
concentration

Audience: kindergarten, primary

Group Size: small or large group

Setting: circle time

Directions: When a quiet break is needed, this game is perfect. A child is selected to be the *Mother* or *Father*. This child sits on the floor across the room from the rest of the group. She or he says, *I have a headache* and covers eyes and head with his or her hands (so as not to be disturbed). The children walk up very quietly and sit beside the Mother or Father. If the approaching child is heard, the Mother or Father moans, *Ohhh* and points in that player's direction. This child must go back to his or her place across the room and begin again. The game ends when a child successfully sits next to the Mother or Father without being detected and asks, *Are you feeling better?* The Mother or Father replies, *Yes. Thank you.* The child becomes the next Mother or Father.

Harder: Mother or Father must guess who is sitting next to to him or her by listening to the child's voice.

Variation: *Silent Circle*   One child sits in the center of a circle with his or her eyes shut. You point to a player who tries to sneak up to the center child without being heard. All of the other players remain silent. If the center child hears a sound, he or she points in that direction. The player returns to the circle and another player is selected. The designated player attempts to touch the center child without being detected. Play continues until one child finally sneaks up and touches the center child. This child then sits in the center with eyes shut and the game begins again.

Traffic light

Develops: listening skills
action-word coordination
awareness of symbolism
awareness of roles
counting skills (H)
gross motor skills
impulse control

Audience: toddler (E), preschool (E),
kindergarten, primary

Group Size: pair (E), small or large group

Setting: playground, gym, imaginative play,
social studies, language, math (H),
movement

Directions: Help children become aware of traffic safety rules with this amusing but educational game. One child is the *Police Officer*. The rest of the children pretend that they are each driving a car. Have them line up on the starting line facing the Police Officer, who is at least fifteen feet away across the playground or gym. When the Police Officer yells out, *Green light!*, the cars move forward. If the Officer says, *Yellow light!* they proceed cautiously and slowly. When the traffic controller cries out, *Red light!* all of the cars must come to an immediate stop. Any cars in motion after the call, *Red light!*, are sent back to the starting line to begin again. The driver who reaches the Police Officer first becomes the next traffic controller.

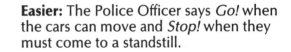

Easier: The Police Officer says *Go!* when the cars can move and *Stop!* when they must come to a standstill.

Harder: *Red Light*   Instead of calling out traffic light colors, *It* begins to count up to ten. At any time, the leader may add *Red light!* as a sign for the players to stop.

Variation: The play continues until all of the cars arrive safely at the finish line.

Adaptation: For hearing impaired children, or as a game variation, the traffic controller uses hand signals with, or without, spoken instructions.

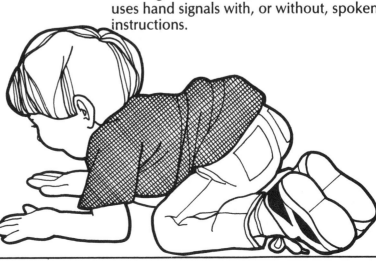

Letter, word, and number games sharpen reading, writing, spelling, and math readiness skills. In this chapter, traditional counting and alphabet games, fingerplays, songs, rhymes, and chants are introduced for good old-fashioned fun. Number concepts and number problems are explored during game-play. Pre-writing activities are provided that use small fingers as writing tools. Games are played which enable the children to become familiar with beginning sounds, letters as visual symbols, and identifying letters.

Parents and teachers often feel pressure for the children to learn how to read or add and subtract. These games are designed to help make these experiences enjoyable, rather than stressful.

The name game

Develops: discrimination of letters/names
self-awareness
listening skills
motor skills
thinking skills
group consciousness

Audience: toddler (E), primary (E), kindergarten, primary (H)

Group Size: pair, small or large group

Setting: language, circle time, transition (E), snack (E), self-awareness

Directions: The leader says, for example: *I see someone whose name begins with P.* Those children stand up. The leader states more specific directions: a particular type of person or a style of locomotion, for example: *All of the boys whose names begin with P, hop up and down three times!*

Easier: *Pat-a-Cake* The players can dramatize this nursery rhyme by substituting a beginning letter and a specific child's name. The child feels so special when his or her name is mentioned. Here's an example:

> Pat-a-cake, pat-a-cake, baker's man.
> Bake me a cake as fast as you can.
> Pat it and prick it
> And mark it with an R,
> And put it in the oven
> For Roberta and me.

Harder: *A, My Name is Alice* is a classic jump rope jingle. Each player is assigned a letter of the alphabet. The child fills in information for a female or male name: the *name of a husband or wife, a location,* and *an item for sale.* Each time the game is played, the responses are creative and unique! Here is an example: *L my name is Lillian; my husband's name is Lee. We live at Lake Dunmore where we sell Lambs.*

Adaptation: For the child who has a poor self-image, these games allow him or her to shine. Select the child after the others have had a few turns, so that he or she will feel comfortable with the directions.

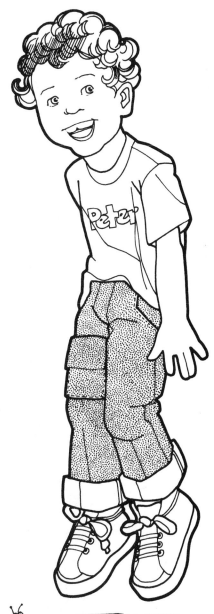

Let's go shopping

Develops: classification skills
language development
beginning phonetics
memory
thinking skills
listening skills
awareness of jobs and roles

Audience: preschool (E), kindergarten (E), primary

Group Size: pair, small or large group

Setting: at desks, circle time, snack time, social studies, language

Directions: Select a shopkeeper and pick a specific letter of the alphabet. The players, one at a time, try to think of items sold in the store that begin with the named letter. For example, the shopkeeper says: *Let's go shopping. I am a butcher and I sell things that begin with the letter H.* The players state items such as: *hot dogs, hamburgers,* and *ham.* The players continue until they cannot think of any more responses. They may then start again with the same shopkeeper and a new beginning letter, or change both the shopkeeper and the letter.

Easier: A specific type of store is named. The players name general items sold in this store, for example: *I own a toy store and sell dolls, games, and blocks.*

Harder: Name a letter that has more than one sound (C, G, I, and so on), for example: *I am a baker and sell things that begin with C: cakes, chocolate cupcakes, cinnamon buns, and cream puffs.*

Variations: 1. This is a spin-off of the game, *In Grandmother's Trunk I Packed.* The name is *In My Shopping Bag I Packed*. One player names an item. The second player repeats the first and names a new item. Each successive player lists all of the other players' items in order, then adds another. 2. Name a special shopkeeper. Each player, in turn, names an item beginning with the next letter of the alphabet. *I am a produce vendor and I sell apples.* For a change, it's fun to begin with a letter in the middle of the alphabet or start with Z and work backwards to A.

Adjective abc

Develops: oral communication
creative thinking
alphabetical sequencing
listening
memory (H)

Audience: primary

Group Size: small or large group

Setting: language, circle time, traveling, dramatics (V)

Directions: The players pick any common object that is easy to describe, for example: *a house*. Going around the circle, the players must think of adjectives in alphabetical order that describe the item. Here are some possible descriptive words: *adorable house, beautiful house, cute house*. Give hints if necessary. A player may pass if he or she cannot think of an adjective.

Harder: *The Minister's Cat*   The children use adjectives in alphabetical order to describe *the Cat*. Each time an adjective is added, the next player must list all of the others before he or she adds another. For example, the third player may say: *The minister's cat is an amusing, brave, cuddly cat*. When a player is stumped, the next player in the circle repeats the letter.

Variation: *Adjective Mime*   After the players have selected an item, such as *hands*, they mime adjectives in alphabetical order which describe the object. The first child might pantomime *angry hands* for the group to guess. The second player could act out *big* hands.

Window abc

Develops: alphabetical sequencing
letter recognition
beginning phonetics
visual discrimination
simple choice-making
oral communication
listening skills

Audience: late kindergarten (V), primary

Group Size: pair or small group(s)

Setting: language, circle time, traveling

Directions: There are many, many ways to play this game. The players sit near a classroom window and look outside for items. Or, as students walk on a field trip, have them observe objects in a store window. This is also an excellent traveling game—have children watch out the vehicle's windows for specific items. To play, children work as a group to locate and name objects (in alphabetical order) that can be seen through the window. Some items along the way might include: *A—automobile, B—bus, C—church*. If the children cannot locate an item which begins with the letter, they begin again, or skip that letter. Divide a large group into teams.

Variations: 1. Pick a specific letter of the alphabet and count how many items can be observed that begin with that letter. Look at how many possible T words can be found: *tree, truck, traffic light, telephone pole!* Try other letters of the alphabet. See which letter has the most items.
2. Look at signs, posters, billboards, or other printed items; attempt to compile the alphabet by pointing out words that begin with the appropriate letter: *A—avenue, B—bank, C—crossing*.

Adaptation: Another game variation for the entire group can be successfully played by the visually impaired child. Open the window and *listen for alphabetical sounds: A—automobile driving by, B—beep of a horn, C—chirp of a bird.*

Letters in a line

Develops: recognition of alphabetical order
organizational skills
problem solving
memory
awareness of actions and positions
sequencing skills

Audience: primary

Group Size: small (at least three players)
or large group

Setting: language time, math (V)

Directions: Three players line up and face the group. The middle child thinks of a specific letter. The player to the right of the middle child has to determine the letter that comes before the middle player's letter. A possible exchange may go like this: the middle child selects the letter S. The child to the right then announces, *I am an R because I come before S*. The student to the left of the middle player must then say, *I am a T because I come after S*. The class confirms the validity of the players' statements.

Easier: Assign each of three players a letter (T,R,S). They arrange themselves in alphabetical order (R,S,T).

Harder: Give the three players letters spaced apart (R,S,V) to arrange in alphabetical order.

Variations: Play the game using other sequences—for example, *numerals (ordinal and cardinal) or dates (days of the week or months of the year)*.

Spelling chain

Develops: oral communication
thinking skills
auditory discrimination
awareness of others' responses
simple choice-making
spelling skills

Audience: primary

Group Size: pair, small or large group

Setting: circle time, language, traveling

Directions: The first player spells a word. Each player in the circle in turn spells a new word that begins with the final letter of the last word. Here is an example of the chain: *bat, tan, nut.* If a player cannot spell a word, the chain ends. Begin again with the next player spelling a new word.

Easier: *Telling Chain*   A word is chosen. The next player tells a word that begins with the ending sound of the previous word. If a word ends with a silent letter, the child gives a word that begins with the letter he or she heard last. (Or the group may decide ahead of time to enforce strict spelling rules! In this case, a word beginning with the silent letter must be used).

Variation: The first player determines a category and spells or tells a word belonging to it. In turn, the players spell or tell a new word which starts with the final letter of the last word. For example, the category is *names*. The sequence may go something like this: *Sean, Ned, Dolores.*

Spelling baseball

Develops: spelling skills
listening skills
turn-taking
sequencing skills
competition
math computation (V)

Audience: primary

Group Size: at least twelve players for two teams

Setting: language or math

Directions: The players form two teams. Each team selects a pitcher and an umpire. The players for one team receive the spelling words from the other team's *Pitcher*. After the Pitcher *pitches* the word, the first player to bat tries to spell it. The umpire holds the spelling book to check the weekly review spelling words for accuracy. If the batter spells correctly, the player walks to an area designated as *first base*. If the batter misses the word, the *Umpire* calls the player out. The Pitcher continues with new spelling words. When four players have spelled words correctly and moved around the *bases*, a run is scored. When three outs occur, the next team comes up to bat. If one team is running up the score, assist the pitcher by increasing the level of difficulty. If the teams wish, games may be played weekly to determine a *World Series Champion*.

Variation: The Pitcher substitutes math problems for spelling words. (This is an entertaining way of practicing multiplication tables.)

Trace and guess

Develops: recognition of letters, words,
numbers, or shapes
directionality
fine motor skills (writing)
concentration
alertness to sensory clues

Audience: toddler (V,A), preschool (E),
kindergarten, primary (H)

Group Size: pairs, small group

Setting: lap, circle, desks, reading or
math group, writing

Directions: Children work in pairs, or one
child stands with his or her back to a small
group. Using a predetermined category, the
challenger traces a letter, number, or shape
on another child's back with a finger. (It's
O.K. to giggle!) The guesser must say what
he or she thinks the strokes represent.
Reverse roles; the other child traces, while
the first guesses. If playing in a small group,
the children may verify the guesser's
answer.

Easier: The challenger traces a line on a
youngster's back. The child guesses the
direction: *up, down, all around, high* or
low, and *top* or *bottom*.

Harder: The challenger traces a word, such
as a spelling word, on the guesser's back or
uses two numbers for addition or
subtraction responses.

Variation: The guesser closes his or her
eyes. The challenger traces a finger line on
various body parts—an arm, a leg or a
nose. The guesser tells where he or she was
touched.

Adaptations: 1. With a young child, or one
who needs special nurturing, hold the child
in your lap as you trace a line on his or her
back. What a wonderful way to tickle and
laugh the afternoon away!
2. For the bilingual youngster, or one who
needs extra practice or stimulation, hold
the child's tracing finger and say the letter,
shape, or number, as you trace on your arm
or on his or hers.

Skywriter

Develops: visual discrimination
action-word coordination
gross motor skills
thinking skills
decoding skills
writing skills

Audience: kindergarten (E), primary

Group Size: pair, small or large group

Setting: circle time, language (spelling),
math (V), dramatics, writing

Directions: The players face the front of the room. A *Skywriter* comes up to the front of the room and stands with his or her back to the group. With exaggerated large motions, the Skywriter *writes* a word high in the air using the pointer finger for the Airplane while the players observe. When a player can identify the word, he or she pronounces and spells it for the group. This child becomes the next Skywriter. This game is an excellent way to have fun practicing new spelling words.

Easier: The Skywriter writes a single letter, number, or shape for the group to identify.

Variations: 1. The Skywriter writes a special letter. After the players guess the letter, they must tell words that begin or end with this letter.
2. After the Skywriter traces a number, for example, 6, the rest of the players give combinations that equal the number: *2 + 4, 3 + 3, 1 + 5.*

Adaptation: Take the visually impaired child's hand and copy the Skywriter's forms with the child so that he or she can guess the answer.

Body letters/numbers

Develops: concepts of letters/numerals
body awareness
cooperation
problem solving
gross motor skills
coordination
improvisation

Audience: late preschool (E), kindergarten, primary (H)

Group Size: pair, small or large group

Setting: language, math, circle time, movement, self-awareness, dramatics, gym, playground

Directions: Call out various letters. The players manipulate their bodies to form the letters. Certain letters are appropriate for one child to create alone by using body, arms, or legs (O, S, F, Y). Other letters can be formed by two or three children working together (Q, B, N). Allow the players to work where they feel comfortable, on the floor or standing.

Easier: Arrange selected players' bodies to form a specified letter. The others guess the letter.

Harder: Offer a spelling word. The children create the first letter of the word. For a greater challenge, small groups of players work together. Their bodies spell out the entire word.

Variations: 1. The leader names different numerals for the players to create with their bodies.
2. Harder: Give number problems to the players (2+2, 6−2 or 2✕2). Ask them to form the answers with their bodies.

Adaptation: Have a physically challenged child select a letter partner with whom to create the body shapes.

How many?

Develops: alertness to tactile cues
counting skills
concept of sets
language
body awareness
social interaction

Audience: toddler, preschool,
kindergarten (H)

Group Size: pair, small or large group

Setting: diapering, transition, math, circle
time, music (V), language,
self-awareness

Directions: This is a nice game to play while a young child is being diapered or held in an adult's lap. While gently patting a specified body part, talk with the child. Say things such as the following: *How many noses do you have? One! Count with me— one!* Encourage the child to touch the body part, too. After a while, he or she will enjoy patting and repeating, *Nose: One.*
Next, point to the many body parts that usually come in *twos: legs, ears, hands and knees.* Play the game by counting and having the child touch and count with you. This game lends itself well to lots of giggling and snuggling!

Adaptation: If English is a second language for the child, pat the body parts and say the names in both languages to help the child learn the words. This is an excellent game for the physically challenged to play. Pair him or her with another child to form the letters or numbers.

Harder: After the children have had many experiences in counting, have them tell the body parts that can be counted by *one.* Increase the level of difficulty by naming body parts that come in *twos, fives,* or *tens.* For added merriment, have the respondent point out his or her answers on a friend.

Variation: Sing and dramatize the traditional song, *The Hokey Pokey* (page 21), by putting *one tummy in* or *two elbows in.*

One potato

Develops: practice in counting
action-word coordination
directionality
motor skills
visual awareness
imagination

Audience: toddler (E), preschool,
kindergarten (H,V),
primary (H,V)

Group Size: pair, small (V) or large group

Setting: math, dramatics (H), circle time,
transition, language (H)

Directions: This old-fashioned counting game is an outstanding game for children to strengthen hand-eye coordination. To play, have youngsters form their fists into *potatoes*. The children stack the potatoes one on top of another climbing up to the sky, chanting:

> One potato, two potato,
> Three potato, four.
> Five potato, six potato,
> Seven potato, more!

Easier: Young children love to pile the potatoes as you repeat the rhyme!

Harder: The children decide what kind of potatoes their fists are before counting them one on top of the other: They can be *hot, cold, heavy or gooey* mashed potatoes. Have them dramatize each type as they count and pile them.

Variation: *Hot Potato*   The players sit in a circle holding their fists out in front of them. Choose a leader to gently hammer each extended fist with his or her own. (This is done while the group rhythmically chants the number rhyme.) When a fist is tapped on the word *more*, the player places it behind the back and play continues. When only one person has a fist held out, the game starts again. This person is the *hot potato.*

Good night!

Develops: number concepts
group consciousness
imagination
sequencing skills
listening skills
a sense of humor
gross motor skills

Audience: preschool, kindergarten, primary (H)

Group Size: small or large group

Setting: math, dramatics, circle time, language

Directions: *Move Over*   This number game can be played with all of the children in a small group. If the group is large, repeat the game several times to give everyone a turn. One child lies down in the center of the circle, which is the *bed* at the beginning of the song. Point to another child to squeeze next to him or her each time the group singing indicates that another child should climb in bed. (Repeat the first three lines as many times as desired, then finally chant *Good night!* At the end, all of the youngsters *snore*! The children love the silliness of this chant.

> There were (number) in the bed
> And the little one said,
> Move over, move over.
> Good night!

Harder: *Roll Over*   This number chant requires the players to count backwards. Start with the desired number of children resting closely together on the floor in *bed*. This group may also want to add funny *snoring sounds*. On *roll over,* a child rolls out of bed so that there is one fewer each time. Repeat the first four lines until only one child is left in the center. Then everyone says the last two lines. The child who's left says *Good Night!*

There were (number) in the bed
And the little one said,
Roll over, roll over.
So they all rolled over and one fell out.
There was one in the bed
And the little one said,
Good night!

Take away rhymes

Develops: concept of numbers
fine motor skills
listening skills
reversibility (E)
visual discrimination
action-word coordination

Audience: toddler (E), preschool,
kindergarten, early primary

Group Size: pair (E), small (E) or large group
(at least ten) (H)

Setting: math, circle time, dramatics,
transition, snack (H)

Directions: Children's first experiences with numbers usually relate to counting exercises. Here is a new twist that also introduces the players to subtraction as the characters are taken away.

Easier: *Two Little Blackbirds*   To begin, make two fists, then hold up the index fingers. At the second line, wiggle left then right fingers. For the third line, place first the left, then the right hands behind the back. In the last line, bring the left, then right fingers in front, and begin again!

> Two little blackbirds sitting on a hill.
> One named Jack and one named Jill.
> Fly away Jack! Fly away Jill!
> Come back Jack! Come back Jill!

Harder: *Ten Sausages*   Begin the verse. Hold up ten fingers. As you say the third and fourth lines, put one finger then another, down. Repeat the verse, substituting *eight fat sausages*. Subtract one finger at each of the appropriate places in the last lines. Continue repeating the verse with *six*, then *four*, then *two* fat sausages, until none are left. And, begin again!

> Ten fat sausages
> Sitting in the pan.
> One went, Pop!
> Another went, Bang!

Variations: 1. Substitute children's names to personalize the rhymes.
2. Ten children lie on the floor, which is the *pan*. Two pop out of the pan each time until there are none left. The chanters clap their hands on *pop* and *bang*.

Who stole the cookies?

Develops: counting skills
sequencing skills
role alternation
rhythm
problem-solving
listening skills

Audience: primary

Group Size: small group

Setting: math, circle time, snack time,
traveling, language

Directions: *Who Stole the Cookies?* The players sit in a circle. A child is selected to be *Number One*. The player on the right is *Number Two*. The children clap their hands to the rhythm of this traditional chant as they repeat the dialogue. The entire chant is repeated with the next number. The players never do discover who stole the cookies from the cookie jar, which is part of the charm of this chant. It's fun for them to guess who the culprit might be—maybe a bear climbed in the window, the dog ate them, or the baker forgot to cook them!

Group: Who stole the cookies from the cookie jar?
Group: Number (One) stole the cookies from the cookie jar.
Number (One): Who, me?
Group: Yes, you!
Number (One): Couldn't be.
Group: Then who?

Variation: Instead of using numbers, the players substitute each others' names in the chant. It is a good get-acquainted game at the beginning of the year that leads to lots of giggling!

A stand-up story

Develops: awareness of numbers
listening skills
action-word coordination
gross motor skills

Audience: preschool, kindergarten, primary

Group Size: pair, small or large group

Setting: math, circle time, language

Directions: This activity enables the youngsters to move a bit while sharpening their listening skills. Tell the class a story using lots of numbers. Each time the children hear a word for a number in the story, they must stand up. For example: Once upon a time *three* little chickens went out for a walk. Along the way they met *six* bunnies eating *six* carrots. Soon, the farmer's *two* sons brought them some lettuce and ....

Harder: The children stand up only when a specific number is named.

Variation: Different stand-up stories may be told using *animals, foods, people's names, seasons,* or *places.* To vary the game, assign different youngsters to listen for a particular word in the category, and stand up when the word is stated.

Adaptation: The story is told in the native language of children who speak English as a second language. Then the players stand and say the number in English.

Numbers change

Develops: awareness of numbers
gross motor skills
quick reactions
listening skills
the ability to characterize
awareness of role reversal

Audience: kindergarten, primary

Group Size: large group

Setting: playground, gym, classroom, math, language, movement

Directions: All of the players stand in a big circle. *It* stands in the center. The children are given consecutive numbers. *It* takes the last number and then calls out any two of the preceding numbers. These players try to exchange places, at the same time *It* also tries to run to a spot. Whoever is left without a place becomes the next *It*.

Easier: Using the players' own names, *It* calls for the players to exchange places.

Harder: *Category Change*   The players select a category, such as *automobiles, ice cream flavors, farm animals,* or *colors.* Each player selects something that is part of the category, for example, *automobiles: fender, light, horn, brakes,* and so on. The person who is *It* calls out one of the selected items.

Variation: Instead of standing in a circle, the players stand in a line facing *It*. After initially counting off the numbers, they scramble to mix them up. *It* stands about 15 feet away from the line and calls out the numbers to be exchanged. These players try to exchange places, as *It* runs to a spot. The person who is left is *It*.

Birthdays

Develops: concepts of age and months
individuality
positive self-image
listening skills
classification skills

Audience: preschool (V), kindergarten, primary

Group Size: small or large group

Setting: math, language, self-awareness, after a birthday snack (V), circle time

Directions: Children love to celebrate birthdays! It is so special to have your very own day and to grow taller and older each year, just like daddy or a favorite big sister. The following rhyme enables the youngsters to share their important birthday month with their friends. When you point to a player after the word *comes,* he or she tells his or her *birthday month.* This child points to the next birthday child as the rhyme continues.

Apples, peaches, pears and plums,
Tell me when your birthday comes!

Easier: After the word *comes,* you name a birthday month. All those children with birthdays during that month stand up. For added fun, see which month has the most birthday children.

Variation: While celebrating a child's birthday, ask other children to raise their hands if the children are: *the same age, older, younger, a year older, two years older, a year younger,* or *two years younger.* This game is always met with great enthusiasm. The players identify with others of the same age!

Adaptation: For the youngster with a poor self-image, celebrating his or her birthday with a group makes the day especially noteworthy; the child feels very special.

Number tricks

Develops: number concepts
language
concepts: more/less, singular/
plural
problem-solving
listening skills

Audience: late preschool (E-1), kindergarten
(E-2), primary (H)

Group Size: pair, small or large (H-2) group

Setting: math, circle time, transition (E),
language

Directions: Children are fascinated with
numbers. It begins the moment that they
can count or hold up three fingers in
response to the question, *How old are you?*
The following games enable the youngsters
to explore numbers as they perform tricks.

Easier: 1. *Singular or Plural*   After exploring
body parts *(one ear, two ears)* or articles of
clothing *(hat, hats)*, help the children to
understand that often an *s* is added to the
end of words to express *more than one* or a
plural. For example, point to your nose.
How would the players tell you that you
have *more than one?* The answer is by
adding an *s* to the end of the word nose.
2. *More or Less*   Begin by holding up two
sets of fingers (two fingers, one finger).
Which is more? Which is less? Later, ask
questions: *Jayson has four crayons and Rosa
has three crayons. Who has more? less?*
Have advanced players tell *how many*
more or less.

Harder: 1. *Give Me Five*   How many ways
can the children brainstorm to express *5?*
(2+3, 1+1+1+1+1, 7−2, 1×5). Have
one child keep score.
2. *Odd or Even?*   The children in the circle
are assigned numbers. The leader calls a
number. The player who has that number
says, *Odd* or *Even*, depending on his or her
number. A player who misses becomes the
new leader. All of the players then quickly
exchange numbers. At times the leader
yells, *Odd* or *Even.* On *odd* the children
with odd numbers stand. On *even* the
children with even numbers must stand.

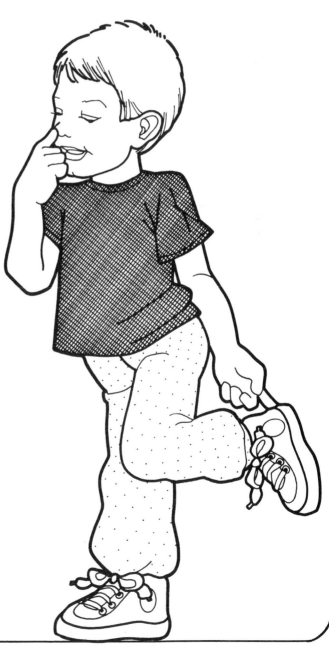

Number please

Develops: concept of numbers
listening skills
memory
sequencing
imagination
communication

Audience: late preschool, kindergarten, primary (H,V)

Group Size: pair or small group

Setting: math, imaginative play, traveling, circle time

Directions: After dialing a make-believe telephone, a child mimics, *Ring-a-ling.* A second child plays the *Operator,* who picks up another pretend phone and says, *Number please.* The Caller tells the Operator a series of numbers. (The amount of numbers in the series may be increased for difficulty.) The Operator attempts to repeat the numbers. This game may be played by pairs who switch roles or one operator and a small group of players who try to trick the switchboard operator.

Harder: After the caller tells the Operator the series of numbers (7-1-4), the Operator attempts to place the numbers in the correct numerical order (1-4-7).

Variation: When the Caller says the series of numbers, the Operator quickly *adds* the numbers to give the Caller a sum. The Caller's numbers can also be *subtracted, multiplied,* or *divided* by the Operator.

Adaptation: To play with the child who speaks English as a second language, a caller relates the number series in one language, while the Operator gives it in English.

Fingers

Develops: concept of numbers
counting skills
visual discrimination (matching)
action-word coordination
problem solving
simple choice-making
fine motor skills

Audience: toddler (E), preschool,
kindergarten, primary (H,V)

Group Size: pair or small group

Setting: math, circle time, transition,
traveling

Directions: Display several fingers. The other players try to match the same number of fingers. Use two hands when the children are ready for a greater challenge. After they have matched the number, the youngsters count their fingers.

Easier: Play as a pair with a child. Allow the child to place his or her fingers over yours for visual and tactile checks. Frequently reverse roles.

Harder: Call out a number. The players must show the correct number of fingers. Using two hands enables the students to show a variety of addition factors.

Variation: *Odd or Even* Children play as pairs. One selects *odd* and the other *even*. They both place one hand behind their backs. A third child says, *Go!* The two put their hands in front of them with one or two fingers extended. A combination of 1+1 or 2+2 renders the even player the winner; 1+2 or 2+1 allows the odd player to win. Use this game for children to select who goes first in other activities.

Adaptation: Have the visually impaired child feel the fingers to match them.

Number looby loo

Develops: number concepts
sequencing skills
action-word coordination
familiarity with a simple melody
problem solving
motor skills

Audience: preschool (E), kindergarten, primary (H)

Group Size: pair, small or large group

Setting: math, music, circle time, gym

Directions: Holding hands, the children form a circle. They walk to the right and sing the chorus of the traditional music fingerplay. The players stop walking, continue to sing and follow the directions in the second stanza. To make this game *Number Looby Loo*, the players substitute a specific number of fingers as they sing each verse. For example: *I put seven fingers in.* For young children, it is simplest to count in order.

Here we go Looby Loo,
Here we go Looby Light,
Here we go Looby Loo,
All on a Saturday night.

I put my right hand in;
I put my right hand out;
I give my hand a shake, shake, shake,
And turn myself about. Oh!

Easier: The players substitute body parts as they sing each verse: *I put one head in* (or two feet, or two elbows, and so on).

Harder: Name a numeral. The players hold up the appropriate number of fingers in the verse. This can also be played with pairs of players showing the numbers with their fingers.

Adaptation: For the bilingual youngster, sing and demonstrate the numbers and words for body parts in both the native language and English.

Moving with numbers

Develops: concept of numbers
counting practice
concept of time
listening skills
action-word coordination
sequencing skills

Audience: preschool (E), kindergarten, primary

Group Size: small or large group

Setting: playground, gym, math, transition (E)

Directions: *What Time Is It, Fox?* The children must be able to count to 12. Discuss the hours on the clock with the players. Establish that midnight is very late, a time for children to be home in bed! The *Fox* stands in the *den* behind a designated line which is 30-40 feet across from the players who are facing him or her. The group calls out, *What time is it, Fox?* The Fox quickly responds with a time. The players move that many steps. The youngsters continue to ask the question and the Fox responds. When the children begin to get close, the Fox answers, *Midnight!* All of the children try to run back behind the line without getting tagged. If a child is caught, he or she becomes the next Fox.

Easier: To make transitions challenging and to maneuver the group from one activity to another, tell the youngsters, for example: *Move with one hop. Move with three skips. Move with two gallops. Move with four leaps.* The children can also suggest ways to move.

Adaptation: The group counts their steps out loud. This gives the child who speaks English as a second language practice in counting.

MIND EXPANDERS

The sky is the limit! Many of the mind expanders in this chapter allow the youngsters to become inventors as they develop novel ideas or find new solutions to problems. The children learn to make decisions while sharing ideas and brainstorming cooperative efforts. Thinking skills are sharpened when the players ask questions in order to gain information or guess answers from clues. During these games, the children are given a chance to become proficient at organizing their thoughts and verbalizing them.

Wheels

Develops: creative thinking
movement exploration
visual discrimination
body awareness
sharing of ideas
concepts of size, speed, direction
awareness of others' actions

Audience: toddler, preschool, kindergarten (H), primary (H)

Group Size: small (H) or large group

Setting: transition, movement, dramatics, circle time, gym, language

Directions: This is an excellent transition activity, especially if the children have been sitting for a while. Explain that by creating moving circles they are going to make wheels with various body parts. (This works best if the players keep their arms or legs stiff.) Demonstrate various wheels for the players to follow: *rotate giant circles with the arms, tiny circles with the fingers, huge circles with the hands, big circles with the head, medium circles with the right foot, and enormous circles simultaneously with the left foot and right arm.* Encourage the players to think of, explore, and share creative wheel combinations. They may change the direction of their wheels: *forward, backwards, or clockwise,* as well as the *size.*

Harder: *Machines* Have the children work in small groups. Using their bodies, each cluster designs a machine with a wheel that has movable parts. First, one child dramatizes a section of the machine. Next, another child joins in and adds his or her moving part. Other players connect their portions of the machine. Soon the giant machine is assembled in working order. The group may add sounds created by the machine as it runs. Other children may guess what type of machine it is or the machine itself may explain to other groups what it is used for and how it works. The children frequently redesign the machine and attach new movable parts. This is a very exciting activity—each youngster will love playing the part of inventor.

Adaptation: The wheel activity is a superb means for physically challenged children to practice exercises with their peers in an enjoyable way.

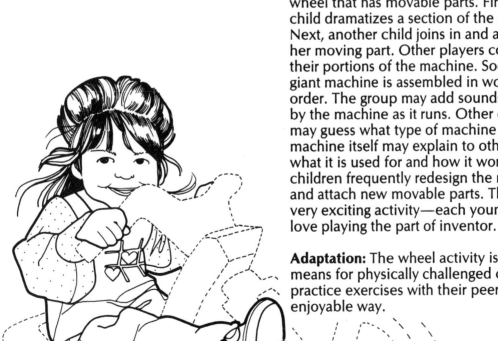

From here...to there

Develops: creative thinking
gross motor skills
action-word coordination
spatial concepts
problem-solving
collaboration
oral communication

Audience: preschool, kindergarten, primary

Group Size: small or large group

Setting: playground, gym, classroom,
language, movement

Directions: Ask the children various movement questions. Encourage them to brainstorm and then demonstrate their solutions. How can they move from: *here to there? (walk, run); as high as they can? (leap, skip); as low as they can? (crawl, scoot, roll); as fast as they can? (run, sprint) or as slow as they can? (go backwards, take baby steps). Encourage both creative and practical responses.*

Easier: Ask the players to respond to familiar, specific problems. For example: *How would they go from the classroom to the school bus?* (Go up the steps, walk down the hall and through the front door.) *How would they go from their house to the supermarket? How would they go from the art easel to the block area?* Encourage the children to be specific about the directions and types of movement.

Harder: Ask the children to respond to abstract problems. For example: *How would they go from Earth to Mars? How would they go from their town/city to Disney World?*

Variation: Form relay race teams to demonstrate some of the solutions offered by the players in the original game.

Opposites

Develops: thinking skills
visual discrimination
gross motor skills
listening skills
concepts of size and position
descriptive characterizing

Audience: preschool, kindergarten, primary

Group Size: pair, small or large group

Setting: circle time, language, movement,
dramatics (V), playground (H)

Directions: *Positions*   To make sure that the children understand various positions, ask them to follow these commands: *Sit on the chair; sit under the chair; sit to the left of the chair; sit to the right of the chair; stand over the chair,* and *go through the chair.* Now request that they listen to the first set of directions, think carefully, and then do the opposite. For example, if you said *sit behind the chair,* the child would sit in front of the chair.

Harder: *Opposite Walk*   Give the players opposite word pairs to explore. While walking around the room, have them discover opposites—*open: a book, a door, a drawer; shut: lid on a paint jar, window, desk top.* Use the game outdoors—*big: a tree, a slide; little: a flower, a beetle.*

Variation: *Sometimes I'm Small*   The players cover their eyes while one child or you chant the following poem. The leader acts out the words, saying *small* with a low, soft voice and *tall* with a high, loud voice. On the last line, the players guess if the leader is *small* or *tall* by the voice used to say *now.* After opening their eyes, the players then stand *tall (hands over head)* or *small (squat down).* A new leader is chosen by the previous one.

Sometimes I'm very, very small.
Sometimes I'm very, very tall.
Sometimes I'm small;
Sometimes I'm tall.
Guess what I am now?

Word wizard

Develops: creative thinking
descriptive characterizing
problem-solving
collaboration
oral communication
listening skills

Audience: primary

Group Size: pair or small group(s)

Setting: language, traveling, circle time

Directions: Present a make-believe word to the children. (Example: chillame) As *Word Wizards*, they create a meaning for the new word for a special dictionary. The players must first determine how the word is to be used: is it an object, an action word, or a descriptive word? The players then try out their word in a sentence. *My chillame (small, green dog) likes to eat puppy chow.* Give each youngster an opportunity to create his or her words and meanings.

Harder: An individual or small group of players use their make-believe words in a story. Another group of *Word Wizards* tries to guess the meaning of the word after hearing the tale.

Variation: The *Word Wizards* try to invent new words which describe things or objects, for example: *an apple—scrumchily* or *flowers— bunchily.*

KER-CHOO-DLE!

Famous sayings

Develops: creative thinking
descriptive characterizing
syntax
oral communication
collaboration
individuality

Audience: preschool (E), kindergarten (E), primary

Group Size: pair, small or large group

Setting: language, circle time, traveling

Directions: Invite the children to design bumper stickers for their favorite activity or a new business. Give them examples to start them off: *Soccer gives me a kick!* or *Archaeologists dig deep.* They may wish to publicize their school or hometown: *Vermont has it all.*

Harder: To extend this activity, select a commercial product and brainstorm bumper stickers or slogans. Send the ideas to the company. The children may have a winner!

Easier: Have each child invent a word or phrase for a personal bumper sticker that tells how each child feels. This game helps you to keep in touch with the children's feelings.

Variation: Each player is provided with an opportunity to think of a word that he or she thinks should become famous and tell why.

Adaptation: Invite a resource person to demonstrate to the players how to sign special words for the hearing impaired. Encourage children to try their hand at sign language.

How many ways?

Develops: divergent thinking
oral expression
creativity
imagination
social interaction
collaboration
common sense

Audience: primary

Group Size: individual, pair, small or large group

Setting: classroom, committees, brainstorming session, language, circle time

Directions: Players work individually, in pairs, in small committees, or as a group. Ask them to list how many ways they can think of to use a newspaper. Encourage the children to brainstorm and be as creative as possible. Sample suggestions might be: *to read*, *to train a puppy*, or *to fold for a hat*.

Easier: Work in committees to elicit cooperative responses.

Harder: Brainstorm, then throw out the first five answers to encourage the children to develop creative responses.

Variations: Play the game using other items, such as a *brick, umbrella, plastic garbage bag, bed sheet, paper bag*, or *dishpan*.

Invent a game

Develops: imagination
divergent thinking
language
sequencing skills
simple decision-making
role awareness
collaboration

Audience: primary

Group Size: individual, pair, small or large group

Setting: indoors or outdoors, brainstorming session, language

Directions: Explain to the group that you have just received new equipment, *two pails, a beach ball, four jump ropes,* and *a scooter.* Ask the children to design a game to play outdoors on the playground. Guide the class with such questions as: *Will you need teams? How many players? What about rules? How long will the game be played? What determines how the game ends and who wins?* Have them try playing their games on the playground with real equipment.

Harder: Add an imaginary object with a silly sounding name (e.g. *wiggly poof*) to the original pieces of equipment. The children first have to determine how it is used before it can be incorporated into the new game.

Variation: Present the same game design information to several small groups of children. After brainstorming, have the groups share their ideas. Are they similar or different? To make this harder, give each group a different quality or condition to consider in designing the game. For example, explain that the *weather* is different: one group must design the game for play in *rain* ; one for play in *sunshine* ; and another, in *snow* . Or, you might tell one group the game is to be played *in the house* ; another, *in a park* ; a third, *in a pool.*

Easier: Begin with a game that the children have seen played before, for example: football. Change one rule (use four teams or substitute a beach ball). Ask, *How might the game be played differently with the change?*

Tall tales

Develops: creative thinking
problem solving
imagination
notions of fantasy
oral communication
collaboration
sequencing skills

Audience: preschool (E), kindergarten, primary

Group Size: pair or small group(s)

Setting: language, traveling, circle time

Directions: Give the players time to gather their thoughts and use their imaginations. Have them think of an outrageous tale to share with the group. Offer them the option of working in pairs or small groups for a cooperative story. Some children may even enjoy spinning an individual yarn. To add another dimension to this activity, have the children award honors for the *funniest, scariest,* and *wildest* tales. And, make sure that each person who tells a tale receives some special mention.

Easier: Communicate a short story to the participants. After a discussion at the conclusion of the yarn, the players must decide whether it was a tall tale (make-believe) or a story that really happened.

Variation: Start to tell a tall tale and stop in the middle. Each child narrates a different ending to this tale!

Who am I?

Develops: thinking skills
imagination
descriptive characterizing
verbal understanding
awareness of roles

Audience: kindergarten, primary

Group Size: pair, small or large group

Setting: circle time, at desks, dramatics, traveling, social studies, language

Directions: Select one child to be the leader. This child leaves the area or covers his or her ears so that the group's discussion cannot be heard. The group decides on a character *(Snoopy, Humpty Dumpty)* or person *(firefighter, George Washington)* to assign to the leader. When this child returns to the group, he or she asks the other players questions to see who he or she represents. Clues may be given about the mystery person—such as his or her special traits, occupation, duties, and so on.

Easier: Utilize people who are familiar to the child to identify *(mommy, school crossing guard)*. Give lots of hints!

Variation: Select a person and tell the group that this person's name starts with a particular letter, for example: *I am S.* The players ask questions to discover who the mystery person is. The group might ask: *Do you have seven dwarfs?* If the answer is *yes,* a player might guess, *Are you Snow White?* The game continues until the correct answer is guessed.

What if?

Develops: creative thinking
descriptive characterizing
oral communication
problem-solving
individuality
imagination

Audience: preschool, kindergarten, primary

Group Size: individual, small or large group

Setting: circle time, seated at desks,
traveling, social studies, language

Directions: This game helps you to understand how the children are feeling and thinking. Pose situations to the children and ask for their responses. Specific people familiar to the children can be used: *teachers, friends, parents, neighbors,* or *school personnel*. For example, *What if you are your mommy today? How do you feel? What would you do?* Fictitious characters or famous people evoke different types of responses: Santa Claus, Superwoman, Winnie-the-Pooh, Martin Luther King, or Christa McAuliffe. For example, ask a child: *What if you were a rocket pilot for the day? What would you do?*

Harder: 1. Pose abstract situations: *What if you were a baseball bat?* Or, substitute these suggestions: *tree, spring rain, fifty dollar bill,* or *pencil.*
2. Ask the players to brainstorm and solve real situations, for example: *What would you do if: a stranger offered you a ride home from school?, the electricity went off?,* or, *you became lost in a store?*

Variation: Have the children use their imaginations to describe *What if?* Here are some ideas to start you off: *What if...people had two heads? ...grass were purple?* or *...the sun stopped shining?*

Adaptation: Ask a player to think what it might be like if they had a handicapping condition, for example: *What if you could not see? How would your life be the same or different? What if you were Helen Keller?*

Point of view

Develops: creative thinking
descriptive characterizing
problem solving
listening skills
oral communication
awareness of others

Audience: preschool (E), kindergarten (E), primary

Group Size: pair or small group

Setting: language, dramatics (V), circle time, social studies

Directions: Ask the children to close their eyes and imagine that they are a particular thing that you or a leader whisper to them. Have each player open his or her eyes and describe the world around him or her from the point of view of that object. The object might be as general as *a chair* or as specific as *their chair in the classroom*, depending upon the player's level of development. Ask the children to describe *a house* from the point of view of *the front door* or *a football game* from the point of view of *the ball* .

Easier: In a word association game, tell the players a word. They relate a word or phrase to you about what they imagine when they think of this word. Here is an example: the word is *bunny*. The players come up with some of the following descriptive words: *long ears, fluffy tail,* and *hop.*

Harder: Imagine how someone else would handle a situation. State a problem, such as: *a little girl would not share her cookies.* Ask, *How would Cookie Monster handle this? Would Superman handle it the same way?*

Variation: Encourage the players to dramatize their responses to various questions: *How does the ocean appear to a fish?* or *...a rainstorm to a baseball player?* Encourage the children to think of creative responses.

Adaptation: When children tease one another or are unkind, assist them in playing this game using real-life situations. Ask them to see things from the other's point of view: *You just pulled Iris' hair. How do you think she feels right now?*

Fairy godmother

Develops: thinking skills
language
imagination
sharing of ideas
listening skills
simple decision making

Audience: toddler (E), preschool,
kindergarten, primary (H)

Group Size: individual or small group

Setting: language, circle time, dramatics (V),
traveling

Directions: Children each make a wish.
They decide ahead of time whether their
special requests will be *make-believe* (to fly
to the moon on a star) or *realistic* (to meet
Gary Carter at a Mets baseball game). Then
the *Fairy Godmother* waves her wand over
the group and each child is granted one
magic wish. The children explain why the
wishes are important to them.

Easier: *The Fairy Godmother* relates the
children's wishes to an occasion with which
they have had experience, such as: *Wish
for special items to buy on your birthday
shopping spree.*

Harder: The players select or are assigned a
character. They make a special wish, as if
they were that person. For example: *Little
Miss Muffet* wishes for *a spider trap!*

Variation: The players first whisper their
wishes to the *Fairy Godmother*. Then they
pantomime them for the group to guess. If
assistance is necessary, the *Fairy
Godmother* gives hints to the group.

Adaptation: The variation above is a good
participation activity for the hearing
impaired child.

The Midas touch

Develops: creative thinking
language
concept of direction (V-2)
problem solving
sharing of ideas
imagination

Audience: toddler (E,V-2), preschool, kindergarten, primary

Group Size: pair, small or large group

Setting: circle time, dramatics, language

Directions: After explaining the story of King Midas' Golden Touch, ask the children to describe how *they* might use the *Midas Touch*, if they were Kings or Queens. Or, ask them to create and describe their own *Magic Touch*!

Easier: The King or Queen magically touches the players, who turn into a named item. The children should be given time to dramatize the object's actions. The King or Queen may pantomime the item's movements if the children need assistance.

Variations: The King or Queen uses a special touch to make his or her subjects *happy, sad, or angry* . The subjects verbally share something that causes them to feel the specified emotion.
2. *Robot* To make cleanup fun, touch the children to turn them into unique *robots* who follow the controller's commands. This is an excellent activity for children to practice following directional words, such as: *down, up, over, through, under, near,* and *around.*

Food shapes

Develops: thinking skills
language
concepts of shape
sequencing skills (H,V)
awareness of change (H,V)
classification skills

Audience: preschool, kindergarten, primary

Group Size: pair, small or large group

Setting: language, snack time, circle time, science, transition, traveling, math

Directions: The children become very excited when they play this game because they discover that they can think of many items to make quite a long list. Present categories, then ask the players to name items, for example, foods that are round (*an apple, hamburger*) or square (*cracker, a sandwich with the bread crusts cut off*). A more difficult example to give is a triangular type of shape (*slice of pizza, sandwich that has been cut in half diagonally*). Four-year-old Morgan selected her own category of ovals: *watermelon, grapes, raisins, an egg,* and *sort-of an ear of corn*! Other children have determined foods that have a pointed shape (*long pickle slice*) or a shape with holes (*bagel, swiss cheese, doughnut*).

Easier: Play the game during snack or lunch when the children can actually look at the food items.

Harder: See how many foods the youngsters can describe that change shape or form through heating (*apples— applesauce, apple pie*), freezing (*water— ice cube*) or processing (*potato—sliced and fried*, it becomes a *potato chip*). This game is a wonderful follow up to a popcorn party!

Variation: Encourage the children to share a special recipe in which a food becomes a specified shape. Favorite *round recipes* are ones for *cookies, pancakes,* and *fried eggs.* Have them describe oven temperatures, cooking times, and directions. These answers are often very imaginative!

Categories

Develops: language
visual discrimination
classification/characterization
thinking skills
listening skills

Audience: toddler (E), preschool,
kindergarten, primary (H,V)

Group Size: pair, small or large group

Setting: circle time, seated at desks,
transition, snack time, traveling,
language

Directions: Name a general category, such as: *ways to move* or *things to eat.* The rest of the group tries to name things in that category. Present specific categories to offer the players greater challenges: *flavors of ice cream, car models,* or *foods that are red.* Personalized funny responses will be shared, for example: *items served on a hamburger* or *choices of pizza toppings.*

Easier: State categories of items visible to the child: *toys, things we wear,* or *round objects in the room.* The children may touch and say the items.

Harder: After naming a particular category, have the players list things beginning with a specific letter. For example, if the category is *sports* and the letter B is chosen, the children list *baseball, bowling,* and *basketball.* Hints may be given.

Variations: 1. Name things in a particular category (*boat, train, car*). The players guess the category (*transportation*).
2. Use categories from current units or themes of study: *things to bring to the beach, ways to say 6 (5+1, 0+6), animals that live on the farm,* or *things that are hot.*

Adaptation: For the bilingual child, give the response in both languages. Use the easier version above. Touch the item and then say the word.

Same game

Develops: creative thinking
descriptive characterizing
classification skills
oral communication
cultural awareness (A)

Audience: preschool (E), kindergarten, primary

Group Size: pair, small or large group

Setting: language, circle time, transition, snack time, traveling, social studies

Directions: This game gives the players an opportunity to think about relationships between objects and describe them. Ask the children questions, such as, *What is the same about an apple and a cracker? (they are food and they crunch when eaten); What is the same about a knife and a fork? (you eat with them, they are sharp, both are made of metal and you hold them in your hand).* It is possible for a variety of answers to be appropriate. Encourage the players to consider *weight, size, color, shape,* and so on, when they give their answers.

Easier: Play this game during snack or lunch when the children are having a firsthand experience with the selected items.

Variations: Pick items that are alike in some way. For example, *a shoe and a sock (worn on the foot).* Then ask children to describe what is different about the items (a sock doesn't have a sole, a shoe does). Use objects such as: *pencil and magic marker, blanket and pillow, doll and ball,* and so on. 2. Present series of things that are the same and tell why one thing is different. Suggestions: pears, peaches, beans, bananas *(beans—not a fruit)* or bread, peas, butter, bagel *(peas—does not begin with the sound of b).*

Adaptations: *Same Game* Utilize pairs such as these: *tortilla and rice cake* or *tepee and igloo* to enhance cultural awareness. Emphasize that all people are the same because they need food, clothing, and shelter.

Partners

Develops: oral communication
thinking skills
visual discrimination
classification skills

Audience: toddler (E), preschool,
kindergarten, primary

Group Size: pair, small or large group

Setting: circle time, snack, traveling,
language

Directions: Certain items seem to go together as partners. As you name an item, the children try to think of its partner. For example, ask: *What belongs with cup?* The children answer, *saucer.* The players may wish to think of their own items with partners. Here are some suggestions: *table* and *chair, toothbrush* and *toothpaste.* This is an excellent game to play during snack or meal time using food-related partners, such as: *rolls* and *butter, salt* and *pepper, knife* and *fork,* and so on.

Easier: Utilize object pairs in the children's immediate environment. For example: *things on their bodies—eyes* and *glasses; shoes* and *socks,* or *items in the classroom—paint* and *paintbrush.* Have the players point to the partners, as they are located.

Harder: 1. Ask the children to name partners within a specific category. Some categories that may be used include: *food—peas* and *carrots, hot dog* and *bun; sports—ball* and *bat, skis* and *poles,* and so forth.
2. Name partner items and have the players give the category. For example: you name *spoon* and *fork* and the children name *silverware.*

Variations: 1. Think of *partner pairs,* such as: *mittens, shoes,* and *ears.*
2. Name *famous people* or *character partners.* The children may come up with such famous couples as *Batman* and *Robin, Little Bo Peep* and *her sheep,* and *Mickey Mouse* and *Minnie Mouse.*

Adaptation: If English is a second language, say the item first in the native language. For visual checks, point to as many partners as possible.

Hot or cold

Develops: language
thinking skills
sensory discrimination
descriptive characterizing
classifying

Audience: preschool, kindergarten,
primary (H)

Group Size: pair, small or large group

Setting: circle time, transition, snack time,
traveling, listening

Directions: This game is especially appropriate to play during meal or snack time. Ask the players to name items that are hot or cold. After eating a hot snack, it is fun for the children to think specifically of *hot foods* , like *soup, cocoa, baked potatoes* or *oatmeal.* Depending upon the level of the players, ask them to immediately think of *cold things.* (You might play the game with this opposite category on another day.)

Harder: Choose the category hot or cold and have a child name various letters of the alphabet. The rest of the players must think of items in the chosen category that begin with the letter named. For example, if the category *cold* is chosen, the children relate items: *I: ice cube; P: popsicle;* and *S: snow.*

Variation: Present other pairs of opposites and ask children to think of items: *sweet/ sour, loud/quiet, hard/soft, fast/slow,* or *big/little.*

Who, what, when, where, and why?

Develops: thinking skills
oral communication
listening skills
reasoning

Audience: toddler (E), preschool,
kindergarten, primary

Group Size: pair, small or large group

Setting: language, circle time, snack time,
seated at desks

Directions: The players think about specific responses to questions that begin with *Who, What, Where, When,* and *Why.* Either ask one child or allow a group to brainstorm answers. Discuss why players may give different answers to the same questions. Format the questions, using the examples below. (Be sure to give children ample time to answer.) For example:
Who? *Who is wearing red shoes? Who helps you when you are sick?*
What? *What will we see at the zoo? What did you eat for lunch?*
When? *When do you eat supper? When do you take medicine?*
Where? *Where do you get your hair cut? Where do we keep our books?*
Why? *Why are you wearing mittens today? Why do we brush our teeth?*

Easier: 1. Ask questions in only one category.
2. Select questions about the children's immediate environment, such as: *Where are the puzzles?* or about the children themselves: *Who is sitting down?* Allow them to verbalize or point.

Harder: Ask for information about concepts, such as: *Where does water come from?*

Variation: Tell a group nonsense story: have the players fill in random words for each question. For example: *Once upon a time, a WHO? (farmer) lived in a WHERE? (closet). He liked to eat WHAT? (pickles) WHEN? (at midnight) WHY? (to make him happy)....and so on.*

What's my line?

Develops: thinking skills
language
imagination
descriptive characterizing
awareness of others
decoding skills
classification skills

Audience: late preschool (V-3),
kindergarten, primary

Group Size: small or large group

Setting: language, social studies,
dramatics (V-3), circle time

Directions: The children frequently see game shows on television and observe players asking and receiving questions, as well as guessing answers. The following games offer children a chance to try their hands at being game show players and panelists.

Variations: 1. Either a small group of children or the class serves as the panel. A player thinks of a specific occupation. The panel asks the player questions that must be answered with a *yes* or *no* in order to try to guess the occupation. Questions may include: *Do you use a machine? (yes) Is it on the ground? (no) Is it used on water? (no) In the air? (yes) Are you a pilot? (yes!)*

2. A player suggests a specific category to the panel. The panel members see how many occupations they can think of that fit the classification. Some typical categories are: *people who keep us safe (firefighter, police officer); people who feed us (farmer, chef); or people who help when we are sick (ambulance driver, nurse); and so on.*

3. A player chooses an occupation to dramatize (*carpenter—pounding with the fist, as if hammering*). The panel attempts to guess the job from the player's actions.

Earth, water or air

Develops: thinking skills
concentration
listening skills
classification skills
oral communication

Audience: primary

Group Size: small group

Setting: circle time, science, traveling, language

Directions: This game requires a great deal of concentration. The players sit in a circle. The first player names one of the three elements, *earth, water,* or *air.* The next player repeats the element, tells an animal associated with that specific element and then states an element for the next player to describe a related animal. The sequence may go something like this: *AIR—butterfly, WATER.* The next player's response might be *WATER— shark, EARTH.* When a child misses, the game begins again. Ask the youngsters to come up with different animals for the categories, instead of repeating ones already given.

Variation: *Tree, Flower, or Bird?* The child in the center of the circle calls out, *Tree, Flower, or Bird .* One of the three names is substituted after bird. The center child might say, *Tree, flower, or bird. TREE.* He or she points to someone in the circle who responds with an answer, *maple.* If the player does not reply with an appropriate answer, he or she becomes the next leader. Vary the last word to keep the players alert.

What happened before?

Develops: thinking skills
oral communication
problem-solving
sharing ideas
sequencing skills

Audience: kindergarten, primary

Group Size: pair or small group(s)

Setting: language, circle time

Directions: Have the children brainstorm a variety of circumstances that might have happened before something occurred. For example, state, *the little boy became lost.* The children brainstorm what happened before: *He wandered away from his sister; he walked along a road.* State: *the tree fell down.* The children respond: *The lady chopped it; lightning struck it.* Use other examples, such as: *the man began to laugh, the water went all over, the power went off,* or *the firefighters arrived at the scene,* and so on.

Easier: Utilize situations that the youngsters might have observed firsthand. State: *your baby sister cried.* They respond: *My mom pulled Kathy's shirt over Kathy's head; or, my cousin pushed Kathy.* You state: *your mom gave you a big hug.* The children might brainstorm: *I ran over to her, or she came to pick me up at nursery school.* Pose a variety of situations and actions. Encourage imaginative responses!!

Variation: Ask for specific information. *What happened before Spot became a dog? (He was a puppy.) What happened before it was a flower? (It was a seed.)*

MIND EXPANDERS

What comes next?

Develops: listening
sequencing skills
understanding of cues
thinking skills
memory

Audience: preschool (E), kindergarten, primary

Group Size: pair, small or large group

Setting: circle time, seated at desks, math transition, traveling, language

Directions: This game entails careful thinking about relationships. Suggest simple sequences for the players to complete: present a number of things in a series; the children tell *what comes next.* Use the following examples, and create your own:
a) *number:* beginning — 1, 2, 3, ?; middle — 6, 7, 8, ? or backwards — 8, 7, 6, ?
b) *alphabet:* C, D, E, ?; Q, R, S, ?; or backwards — Z, Y, X, ?
c) *seasons:* fall, winter, spring, ?
d) *body parts:* eyes, nose, mouth, ears; shoulder, arm, hand, fingers; toes, ankle, leg, knee.

Easier: 1. Provide sequences that the players can visualize. For example, line up three children. Name the first and second. Have the players name the third person in the line.
2. Name only two items in the sequence and have the children complete it: 1, 2, ?; or B, C, ?

Variation: Ask the players to help tell what happens next in sequencing events that are familiar, for example: *First, everyone sits down at the table. Then, they eat lunch. Next, they clear the table,* and so on. Accept a variety of appropriate responses; some suggestions include: *They wash the dishes. They go to take their naps.* Use this game to review activities just accomplished in the classroom, or daily tasks, such as good health habits like hand washing. Recall events during a field trip: *First we watched the bus pull up to the nursery school. Then we put on our jackets. Then we climbed aboard the bus and drove to the zoo.*

Here is a box

Develops: thinking skills
imagination
auditory discrimination
concept of relationships
sequencing skills
oral communication

Audience: toddler, preschool, kindergarten, primary (V)

Group Size: pair, small or large group

Setting: circle time, transition, language, traveling, imaginative play

Directions: This delightful fingerplay encourages the use of thinking skills and imagination! Have children repeat the verse and mimic your hand movements. When saying the first and second lines, cup one hand, palm side up, then place your other hand over it, palm side down. Say the second line, and tell what's inside *(why it's a kitten!)*. After hearing the name, the children make appropriate sounds *(meowing, mewing,* or *purring),* and so on. As you say the last line, lift off one hand. To vary the game, point to a child who names the hidden noisemaker. The child names: *a type of animal, a noisy object,* or any item, serious or silly, he or she can think of! As the children make the descriptive sounds all at one time, tension is released and laughter fills the air!!

> I wonder whatever inside is hid?
> Why it's a (kitten)
> Without any doubt!
> Open the lid and let it come out.

Harder: The leader makes the sound first, then the players guess the animal or object.

Variation: Create a tiny, small, medium-size, or gigantic make-believe box with your hands. The players use their imaginations to think about possible animals, people, or things that could be hidden inside the described box.

CROSS REFERENCES

INDEX